100 NATIVE AMERICANS

WHO SHAPED AMERICAN HISTORY

BONNIE JUETTNER

sourcebooks
eXplore

Copyright © 2003, 2023 by Sourcebooks
Text by Bonnie Juettner
Cover design by Will Riley
Internal illustrations by Eduard Coll
Cover and internal design © 2023 by Sourcebooks

Published by Sourcebooks eXplore, an imprint of Sourcebooks Kids
P.O. Box 4410, Naperville, Illinois 60567-4410
(630) 961-3900
sourcebookskids.com

Originally published in 2003 by Bluewood Books, an imprint of The Siyeh Group, Inc.

Library of Congress Cataloging-in-Publication Data is on file with the Library of Congress.

Source of Production: Versa Press, East Peoria, Illinois, USA
Date of Production: July 2023
Run Number: 5030859

Printed and bound in the United States of America.
VP 10 9 8 7 6 5 4 3 2 1

CONTENTS

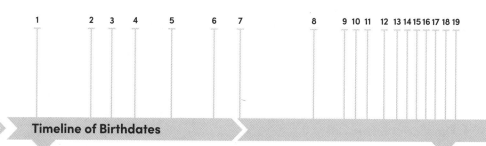

Timeline of Birthdates

1550   1800

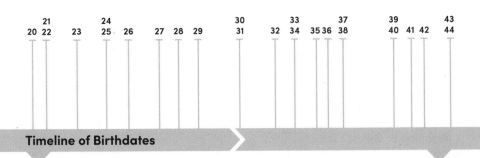

Timeline of Birthdates

1801

1850

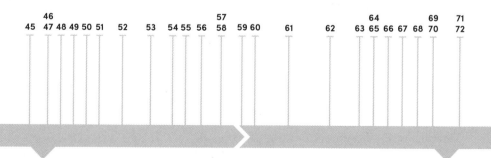

1851

1930

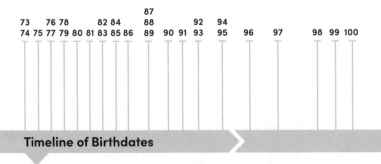

Timeline of Birthdates

1931   1970

INTRODUCTION

HISTORY HAS shown that when Europeans first came to North America, they did not find an uncivilized wilderness. The area that later became the United States, Canada, and Mexico was home to millions of people speaking hundreds of languages. In the years after European contact, more than 90 percent of Native North Americans died in epidemics, and many more were to perish in battles and wars. The history of the relationship between the United States and Native American nations is tragic and shameful. However, it is also a story of Native American courage, ingenuity, persistence, and survival.

Many Native American leaders were masters of diplomacy, and they used peaceful strategies, such as negotiation and compromise, to keep their communities safe from European encroachment. **Massasoit**, **Powhatan**, and **Nanye'hi** worked to negotiate and keep peace treaties with the first colonists. As it became obvious that peaceful methods were not enough, leaders such as **Metacomet**, **Pontiac**, **Black Hawk**, and **Tecumseh** turned their skill at diplomacy to building military alliances among Native American nations to protect their land and stop increasing colonial settlements.

Some leaders made a decision to keep the peace with settlers and the young United States at almost any cost. This strategy worked well for **Seathl**, **Washakie**, and **Plenty Coups**, but it did not help **Black Kettle** at all. Others turned to war when peaceful efforts failed. American history, especially the history of the West, is full of stories of courageous Native American war leaders: **Red Cloud**, **Sitting Bull,** and **Crazy Horse** on the Plains; **Cochise** and **Geronimo** in the Southwest; **Chief Joseph** in the Northwest; **Osceola** in Florida. Often these warriors were not defeated militarily, but economically. The Sioux, for example, could not hope to restore their way of life after most of the buffalo were exterminated.

Gradually, most Native Americans were relocated to reservations on poor land. Some leaders, such as **Manuelito**, **Dull Knife**, and **Standing Bear**, however, were able to force the federal government to grant their people a reservation in their traditional territories, although only after many people in their communities had died marching to and living on the reservations the United States had chosen for them.

As the Native American wars of resistance ended, leaders turned their attention to the problem of rebuilding. **Sarah Winnemucca**, **Susette La Flesche**, and **Gertrude Simmons Bonnin** toured the country lecturing and pushing reformers to do something to improve reservation living conditions. **Charles Alexander Eastman**, **Annie Dodge Wauneka**, and **Betty Mae Tiger Jumper** helped their communities by addressing health problems.

Clinton Rickard, **Vine Deloria Jr.**, **Ada E. Deer**, and **John Echohawk** went to law school and entered politics, as lobbyists, activists, or politicians. **Amos Bad Heart Bull**, **Ella Cara Deloria**, **Maria Martinez**, and others devoted themselves to preserving Native American cultural heritages.

At the same time, many Native Americans excelled in nontraditional careers. **Jim Thorpe** and **Billy Mills** became world-famous athletes. **Maria Tallchief** became an internationally known ballerina. **Will Rogers** and **Jay Silverheels** became household names in the entertainment field. **Buffy Sainte-Marie**'s folk songs are sung around the world. **Oscar Howe** and **Pablita Velarde** made names for themselves in the art world.

In the 1960s, the nation turned its attention to the civil rights movement. Activists

David Sohappy, Janet McCloud, and **Ramona Bennett** worked to preserve the fishing rights of Native Americans in the Northwest, while **Dennis Banks** and **Clyde Bellecourt** formed the American Indian Movement to protect the civil rights of Native Americans across the country. Meanwhile, a Native American literary renaissance exploded: **Scott Momaday** and **Louise Erdrich** are recognized among the nation's finest writers.

Through the efforts of all these people—and many others—it's clear that Native Americans have not only survived but prospered, and will continue to shape American history for many years to come.

Nobody is sure exactly during what years **DEKANAWIDA**, the founder of the legendary **Iroquois Confederacy**, lived. However, historians do know several things about his life. Dekanawida was born in present-day Ontario, Canada. Legend states that when he was a baby, his mother dreamed that he would someday destroy their nation, the **Huron**. So she and his grandmother tried three times to drown him, but the morning after each attempt, they woke to find him sleeping peacefully in his mother's arms. Finally Dekanawida's mother resigned herself to raising him to adulthood.

As an adult, Dekanawida crossed Lake Ontario to what later became New York State. There he met **Hiawatha**, an **Onondaga** from a **Mohawk** community, who became his friend and spokesperson. (Legend says that Dekanawida had a speech impediment that made him stutter severely.) Together, they planned to bring peace to the Native American tribes in the area. Then Hiawatha carried Dekanawida's ideas to the Mohawk, **Cayuga**, **Oneida**, Onondaga, and Seneca, who had been fiercely fighting among themselves for years.

Under Dekanawida's plan, the Iroquois Confederacy became famous for its democratic structures and for the dignity and statesmanship of its leaders. Confederacy leaders were commonly known as chiefs, but some historians believe they were more like chairmen.

Chiefs could not promote their own personal points of view. Instead, they had to carefully represent the interests of their communities. If chiefs did not remain faithful to the interests of their communities, they were removed from office.

In his **Great Law of Peace**, Dekanawida gave men and women roughly equal amounts of power in tribal society. While all chiefs were men, they were chosen by women; in special circumstances, however, men could be elected to office by the chiefs themselves. Women owned the land and the soil. Minorities in Iroquois society were protected from discrimination because Iroquois laws were not passed by majority vote. A policy could not become law unless it was agreed upon unanimously. For his role in ending wars between the Five Nations, Dekanawida is often called "**the Peacemaker**."

Iroquois laws and its system of government should sound familiar to Americans. Several founders of the United States—Benjamin Franklin and Thomas Jefferson among them—admired the Iroquois form of government. In 1754 Franklin drew up his Albany Plan of Union, a document designed to unite the thirteen colonies as a federation modeled on Iroquois institutions. Franklin's plan was not ratified, but it later became the model for the Articles of Confederation, the predecessor to the U.S. Constitution.

Dekanawida's Iroquois Confederacy became the most powerful Native American confederation in North America, and lasted for hundreds of years. Dekanawida achieved his goal—he brought the Iroquois tribes a lasting peace.

SQUANTO, also known as Tisquantum, was the translator and guide sent by the **Wampanoag** leader **Massasoit** (see no. 3) to help the **Pilgrims** during their first few years in America.

Historians know little about Squanto's early life. He was a member of the **Pawtuxet** tribe, one of many Algonquian-speaking tribes of present-day New England. Some historians believe that English explorers kidnapped him and took him to England in 1605, and that he returned with John Smith in 1614. After Smith left, Squanto and twenty other Pawtuxet were kidnapped by explorer **Thomas Hunt**. Hunt took them to Spain and sold them as slaves, but Squanto was rescued by Spanish friars. He went to England and began working for English explorers, perhaps as an indentured servant. He traveled to Newfoundland in 1617 and came home to the Pawtuxet area, in Massachusetts Bay, in 1619.

An epidemic had swept through the region in his absence. Squanto found his village abandoned; most Pawtuxet had died or moved away. When his employer was killed in a battle with the **Wampanoag**, Squanto became a prisoner of Massasoit. When the Pilgrims settled Plymouth Colony, Massasoit sent Squanto and another English-speaking prisoner of war, **Samoset**, to talk to them. After Squanto translated as Massasoit and Pilgrim leaders negotiated a treaty, Squanto remained in Plymouth Colony.

Most of the English settlers had not been farmers in England. Squanto taught them how to plant corn and other American vegetables, because their seeds of English barley, wheat, and peas did not thrive in New England. He also taught the colonists how to make fish traps and guided them as they explored the region.

Squanto continued to serve as a translator when the Pilgrims needed to communicate with Massasoit and with other Native American tribes in the area. The Pilgrims were relieved to have Squanto's help. **William Bradford**, one of the Plymouth Colony's governors, described him as "a special instrument sent of God for their good beyond their expectation."

Some historians believe that Squanto was hoping to use his friendship with the Pilgrims to gain political power. He may have hoped to replace Massasoit as the leader of the Wampanoag. In 1621 Squanto told the English that Massasoit was planning to attack the colony. Actually, Massasoit had no plans to attack, and Squanto's lie nearly destroyed the peace between Plymouth Colony and the Wampanoag.

When Squanto's deceit was discovered, Massasoit demanded his execution, but the Pilgrims depended on him so heavily that they protected him from the consequences of his actions. The following year, Squanto became ill and died while he was guiding Bradford on a trip around Cape Cod.

3 MASSASOIT

c. 1590–1661

MASSASOIT, the leader of the **Wampanoag**—one of many Algonquian-speaking tribes in New England—helped the **Pilgrims** survive their first winters in New England. He negotiated a treaty with the new settlers and maintained peace between his tribe and the **Plymouth Colony** throughout his lifetime.

When the Pilgrims arrived in Plymouth, Massachusetts, in 1620, they were not the first Europeans to visit the mainland of North America. John Cabot landed there as early as 1497, Giovanni da Verrazano in 1524, and, just a few years before the Pilgrims, Samuel de Champlain (1605) and John Smith (1614) explored present-day New England. All these Europeans, and others too, brought with them diseases that killed as much as 75 percent of the coastal population.

When the Pilgrims arrived, the Wampanoag were recovering from an epidemic that had killed eleven thousand people, more than half their population. English explorers had also kidnapped Native Americans in New England, sometimes selling them into slavery. The Wampanoag had every reason to suspect the new settlers, and Massasoit sent scouts to watch them from a distance.

However, the Wampanoag needed an ally against their powerful neighbors, the **Narragansett**, who were untouched by the epidemic. Massasoit had his scouts observe the Pilgrims throughout their first winter, when more than half the Plymouth settlers died. In the spring, perhaps realizing that the Pilgrims were too weak to threaten his tribe, Massasoit decided to befriend them. With his translator **Squanto** (see no. 2) to interpret, he negotiated a peace and friendship treaty with the English. The pact called for mutual defense in case either people was attacked by a third party.

Massasoit and the Wampanoag taught the colonists how to plant and cook American crops. Without their help, the colony might not have survived. A few months later, Massasoit and sixty or more Wampanoag came to Plymouth for the first **Thanksgiving** feast. They brought five deer for the meal, which also included wild turkeys, geese, ducks, eels, shellfish, cornbread, succotash, squash, berries, wild plums, and maple sugar.

The alliance between the Pilgrims and the Wampanoag was to be tested many times. As more colonists arrived in Massachusetts, land disputes arose. Sometimes the disputes resulted from cultural misunderstandings. The English sometimes thought they had purchased land outright, when Native Americans had intended only to share the right to use the land. Other times, newly arrived settlers simply moved onto Native American land without permission. Some English settlers raided Native American communities to get food.

Although he lost much of his respect for the English over the years, Massasoit worked hard to keep peace with the colonists. He kept his treaty with the Pilgrims until his death in 1661.

A force for peace between her people and the first English settlers at **Jamestown**, **POCAHONTAS** was the daughter of **Powhatan**, the leader of a league of thirty Algonquian tribes in eastern Virginia. She was born just after the Native Americans in the area had been decimated by epidemics of European diseases, such as measles, bubonic plague, and typhus.

Despite the epidemics, however, the Powhatan were better off than the Jamestown community, which was established in 1607. The Powhatan were efficient farmers and grew plenty of beans, pumpkins, and corn. During the winter of 1608, when the English colonists began to starve because they hadn't planted sufficient crops, Pocahontas brought them food. Legend has it that around this time, Pocahontas also convinced her father to spare the life of English captain **John Smith**, who the Powhatan had captured. However, some historians believe Smith made that story up.

Pocahontas traveled freely among Powhatan villages and the English settlements, and sometimes negotiated with settlers on behalf of her father. When she was thirteen, John Smith took seven hostages after a skirmish between the Powhatan and the colonists. Representing her father, Pocahontas successfully negotiated for their release.

In 1609 relations between the Powhatan and the settlers broke down, and Powhatan planned to attack John Smith's camp. Pocahontas warned Smith, and he and his men were able to escape. However, the Powhatan would no longer trade with or assist the Jamestown settlers.

In 1610 when she was about fifteen, Pocahontas married **Kocoum**, one of her father's allies, and went to live with the **Patawomeck** on the Potomac River. In 1612

Samuel Argall, a Jamestown colonist and sea captain, visited the Patawomeck and kidnapped Pocahontas. Argall hoped that if he held Pocahontas as a hostage, he could persuade Powhatan to release English hostages, guns, swords, and tools. Pocahontas lived in Jamestown for a year. While she was being held captive, she converted to **Christianity** and took the name **Rebecca**. She also met **John Rolfe**, a businessman who had come to Jamestown to grow tobacco. The two fell in love and married in 1614, a move that helped bring about peace between the settlers and the Powhatan. (History does not record what happened to Pocahontas's first husband, Kocoum.) The next few years became known as the "Peace of Pocahontas," and it lasted for the rest of her short life.

In 1616 she traveled to England with her husband and their infant son, Thomas. In London, she was presented to King James I and his queen, who were impressed by her manner and appearance. Pocahontas died of an illness in 1617, just before she and her family were to return home.

◆ **POPÉ** led one of the most successful revolts in Native American history. He and his allies drove the **Spanish** out of the area around **Santa Fe**, in present-day New Mexico, temporarily restoring the **Pueblo's** traditional way of life.

After the Spanish colonized New Mexico in 1598, they attempted to destroy the traditional Pueblo religion and forcibly convert the Pueblo to **Catholicism**. The Pueblo continued to practice their religion secretly, in underground rooms called kivas. Spanish missionaries burned whatever kivas they could find and destroyed sacred religious objects, such as masks. When the Spanish caught Pueblos practicing their religion, they treated them brutally. The Pueblo were often flogged in public, and sometimes the Spanish even executed those who refused to convert. At other times the Spanish cut off the hands or feet of nonbelievers, or sold them into slavery.

While there are no details concerning Popé's early life, it is known that by the 1670s, he had become an important spiritual leader for the San Juan Pueblo. He was whipped at least three times for refusing to become a Christian and proudly exhibited the resulting scars on his back. Popé made no secret of his opposition to Spanish rule.

In 1675 the Spanish seized Popé and forty-six other Pueblo religious leaders. They took the prisoners to Santa Fe, where they hanged three and whipped and jailed the rest. After his release, Popé hid at the Taos Pueblo and planned a rebellion. He convinced many leaders throughout the Southwest to join his conspiracy. The attack took place on August 10, 1680, catching the Spanish by surprise.

After ten days of fighting, the Pueblo forced the Spanish to retreat to El Paso. Popé took control of Pueblo life. He insisted that all Spanish churches and property be destroyed. He forbade the Pueblo to speak Spanish, and required Christian Pueblos to purify themselves by bathing in suds of the yucca plant.

As time passed, Popé became a tyrannical leader. He executed Pueblos who disagreed with him. He was removed from office and then reelected. At the same time, droughts were making life harder for the Pueblo community, and Popé's political alliance began to fall apart.

Popé died in 1690. Two years later, the Spanish reconquered the Santa Fe area. The revolt had two lasting effects. When the Spanish retreated from Santa Fe, they left horses behind. The horses reproduced and their offspring were traded to northern Native American groups. By the mid-1700s, horses had become indispensable to Native Americans living on the Great Plains. In addition, when they returned to Santa Fe, the Spanish did not outlaw the traditional Pueblo religion, which has survived to this day.

◆ **METACOMET**, the son of **Massasoit** (see no. 3), led the Native American resistance against the English colonists in one of the bloodiest wars in American history. The colonists called Metacomet Philip, and the war he led is usually called "**King Philip's War**."

By the time of Massasoit's death in 1661, the balance of power in New England had shifted. Tens of thousands of English settlers now lived in the region. The colonists were no longer dependent on Native Americans for their survival, as they were when Plymouth Colony was first founded. Beginning in the 1640s, waves of settlers pressed farther and farther onto Native American land, and English cattle trampled Native American cornfields. In addition, colonial leaders tried to enforce English laws over tribes in their region.

When he became the leader of the **Wampanoag**, Metacomet tried to preserve the peace that his father had kept for more than forty years. However, Metacomet kept the peace only in order to buy time. He was working to develop a military alliance of **New England tribes** that he hoped could drive the settlers out of the Americas. He is said to have declared, "I am determined not to live until I have no country." He meant that he would rather die fighting than live to see the day when Europeans would finally take all the Wampanoag's land from them.

King Philip's War began in 1675. The **Abenaki**, **Nipmuc**, **Pocumtuck**, and **Narragansett** all joined the Wampanoag as allies. The Narragansett went to war only after the colonists attacked them and killed several hundred men, women, and children.

The fourteen months of war brought tremendous suffering to both settlers and Native Americans. Whole towns and villages were destroyed; six hundred colonists and three thousand Native Americans, including almost all the Narragansett, were killed. At first, it seemed as if the Native Americans might actually drive the English from the continent. However, as time passed, Native American forces began to starve, as crops were burned and the constant movements of the war gave them no time to plant new ones.

In 1676 a colonial force ambushed Metacomet in a swamp and killed him. The colonists beheaded and quartered his body, and placed his head on a stake in Plymouth, where it was displayed for years. The war was basically over. So many Native Americans had died in the conflict that colonist Increase Mather wrote that it was "no unusual thing for those that traverse the woods to find dead Indians up and down..." Many Native Americans fled the area, while the English sold many others into slavery in the West Indies.

◆ **KATERI TEKAKWITHA**, (Kateri Catherine in English), **Lily of the Mohawks**, was the first Native American to be **beatified** by the **Catholic Church.**

Tekakwitha's Algonquin mother had converted to Christianity before being kidnapped by a Mohawk chief who became Tekakwitha's father. When Tekakwitha was four years old, a smallpox epidemic killed her parents and little brother. Tekakwitha barely survived; she lost most of her eyesight, and was left with facial scars. She was adopted by her uncle, an important Mohawk leader who hated Christians, especially the **Jesuits**. In fact, the Mohawk tortured and killed several Jesuits in the years before Tekakwitha was born.

When Tekakwitha was a young girl, three priests visited her village and stayed for three days. Tekakwitha listened to their teachings, and at age twenty, she was baptized and became a Christian; she also decided to remain a virgin. From then on, Mohawk taunted her for refusing to work on Sundays and for refusing to marry. Some felt she was trying to avoid the responsibilities of a married Mohawk woman. Some Mohawk threw rocks at Tekakwitha, and her own family withheld food from her.

Eventually, Tekakwitha began receiving death threats and fled her village. She traveled by canoe to the Catholic mission at Kahnawake. There, she asked the Jesuits for permission to start her own convent. Although the priests were impressed with her piety, they felt she was too recent a convert to take on such a commitment. Tekakwitha did take a vow of chastity, though, and began to subject herself to rigorous physical trials to prove her faith. She ate very little food, and mixed ashes with the food she did eat. Scantily clad, she prayed outside in the middle of winter. She also slept on a bed of thorns and flogged herself with a whip.

Tekakwitha's behavior was so extreme that it alarmed the Jesuits. However, among the Mohawk, people who could endure torture without showing their feelings were greatly respected, and Tekakwitha may have been trying to show that she was worthy of this kind of respect. However, such practices destroyed her health, and she died at age twenty-four.

In 1943 she was declared venerable, the first step toward sainthood, by Pope **Pius XII**. To be beatified as a saint, a candidate must have shown "heroic virtue." Tekakwitha's virtue consisted of refusing to give up her faith, even when it was dangerous to practice it, and living in a community where her faith made her subject to abuse, stoning, and death threats. Catholics consider her actions heroic because they were motivated by faith without concern for her well-being. Pope **John Paul II** beatified Kateri Tekakwitha in 1980 in Rome.

The **Ottawa** chief **PONTIAC** led one of the most important Native American military alliances in North American history.

Pontiac was born around 1720 and was raised as a traditional Ottawa; as a young boy, he learned about the history of his nation, as well as how to hunt and fight.

During Pontiac's youth, the Ottawa traded furs to French traders for guns and bullets. They lived in relative peace with French settlers in the **Great Lakes** region and Canada, where France's policy was to recognize Native American self-rule, territorial rights, and hunting and fishing rights. However, in 1763 France lost the Seven Years War and gave up much of its territory to Britain. The **British** rejected Native American land claims, and allowed settlers to squat on Ottawa lands. These settlers tried to avoid trading guns and bullets to the Ottawa, who had grown to rely on these weapons.

The Ottawa nation had a democratic government. Each village had several

chiefs who could lead only as long as they retained the respect of the people. Pontiac had become respected for his success in battle. He quickly gained enough influence to build alliances with other Native American nations. As the Ottawa and other nations grew unhappier with the British, Pontiac devised a plan.

Pontiac's hope was that Native American nations could unite, and, with help from France, force the British out of the Great Lakes region. He sent messages to nations from Lake Ontario all the way to the Mississippi River, planning a massive surprise attack on British forts in the region. The **Seneca**, **Delaware**, **Shawnee**, **Miami**, **Ojibwa**, and **Missisauga** all joined his alliance.

In 1763 Pontiac attacked the British fort at Detroit, but the British had been warned and the attack failed. Elsewhere, though, Pontiac's allies took over nine British forts and caused one other to be deserted. Only the Detroit fort and Fort Pitt in Pennsylvania remained under British control.

At this point, the British began smuggling smallpox-infected blankets into Native American camps, producing an epidemic among the Delaware, Mingo, and Shawnee. Meanwhile, the allies learned that the war was damaging the fur trade in the Great Lakes area. Finally, Pontiac learned that the French, who he had hoped would join him, had signed a peace treaty with the British in London. Pontiac ended the siege of Detroit, and the alliance began to break up. He signed a peace treaty with the British in 1765. A few years later, he was stabbed to death on a trading trip to Cahokia, Illinois. Historians believe that Pontiac's alliance was the last time Native Americans had a real chance of stopping the westward expansion of European settlements.

HANDSOME LAKE, also known as Sedwa'gowa'ne, "Our Great Teacher," founded the **Longhouse** religion that is still practiced by many **Iroquois** today. He also helped the Iroquois find a way to adapt to the tumultuous changes that occurred in their world during his lifetime.

When Handsome Lake was born, the **Seneca** were the largest and most important member of the Iroquois League. During the French and Indian War and the American Revolution, they sided with Great Britain. Handsome Lake fought in both wars. During the Revolution, colonial militias destroyed Seneca villages, and in 1797, when Handsome Lake was in his sixties, the United States moved the Seneca onto reservations. At the time, a depressed Handsome Lake was in the middle of a four-year drinking binge. By 1799 alcohol poisoning had turned his skin yellow, and one day he was found unconscious. His daughter, believing he was dead, called her family to the house to prepare his body for burial; however, Handsome Lake was still alive. He was in a trance, experiencing a series of visions.

In Handsome Lake's visions, spiritual messengers gave him instructions for how to cure himself and Seneca society. When he recovered, he stopped drinking alcohol and began to preach a message called *Gai'wiio* ("Good Word"). Handsome Lake continued to have visions, and in his teachings, he combined traditional Seneca ideas with the message of **Quaker** missionaries.

He called for strict observance of Seneca religious ceremonies, and emphasized values such as family, community, and the importance of land. Handsome Lake encouraged his followers to change their land use patterns in response to changing circumstances by giving up hunting and becoming farmers. He also advocated abstention from drinking alcohol or practicing witchcraft. These teachings spread among the Iroquois and eventually developed into the Longhouse religion.

Because of these teachings, especially his views on giving up hunting for agriculture, Handsome Lake was opposed by other powerful leaders, particularly one chief named **Red Jacket**. Still, in 1801 Handsome Lake was elected a political leader of the Seneca. He met with President Thomas Jefferson in 1802 to try to persuade him to guarantee the Seneca their land and to stop traders from taking liquor onto the reservations.

A few years later, many of Handsome Lake's followers left him because he persecuted suspected witches. He became popular again in 1812, and persuaded many Iroquois not to fight in the War of 1812.

However, Handsome Lake's teachings were to receive their greatest popularity many years after his death in 1815. His followers published the **Code of Handsome Lake**, based partly on his teachings and partly on Quaker philosophy, in 1850. By the late twentieth century, about one-third of the Iroquois living in New York State had become followers of the Longhouse religion.

10 MOLLY BRANT

c. 1736–1796

MOLLY BRANT is believed to have been the most powerful Native American woman of the late 1700s. The sister of **Mohawk** leader **Joseph Brant** (see no. 12), she was born in a Mohawk village in present-day eastern New York State and grew up in a world that was filled with European influences. Her parents were **Anglican Christians**, and because she read and wrote English, historians believe she may have attended an English school as a child.

When she was in her early twenties, Brant married **William Johnson**, the British superintendent of the British Office of Indian Affairs for the northern colonies. The marriage was a Mohawk ceremony, not recognized by the British, but it was important in cementing the military alliance between the British and some Iroquois nations.

Molly arranged for her younger brother Joseph to attend the school that later became Dartmouth College, and Joseph fought alongside Johnson during the French and Indian War and Pontiac's Rebellion. Joseph later led the Mohawk and other Iroquois nations to support the British during the American Revolution. Molly bore eight or nine children to Johnson, managed his estate, and may have managed the Office of Indian Affairs in her husband's absence. When Johnson died in 1774, Brant was turned away from his estate, but she remained a **British Loyalist**.

When the American Revolution began, Molly became a spy for the British. Like many Mohawks, including her brother Joseph, she believed that Native Americans had a better chance of keeping at least some of their land if colonial expansion could be stopped. Brant was a persuasive voice within the Iroquois Nation, and her influence is believed to have been as important as that of her brother Joseph in convincing some Iroquois tribes to side with the British in the war. In fact, George Washington once wrote of her, "I am afraid her influence will give us some trouble."

She provided the British with information about movements of colonial troops in the Mohawk Valley and carried ammunition to the British before the **Battle of Oriskany** in 1777. Because of her actions, colonial soldiers and their Oneida allies destroyed her house. Brant fled to Fort Niagara, where she continued her intelligence activities.

After the war ended, she moved to Ontario, Canada, with other Mohawk Loyalists. In recognition of her efforts during the war, Britain awarded her an annual pension of one hundred pounds—bigger than the pension given to her brother Joseph, who had been an officer in the British army. She died in 1796, when she was about sixty years old.

NANYE'HI was a legendary warrior and diplomatic negotiator between the **Cherokee** and European settlers. She earned the highest honor available to a Cherokee woman in her day, the title of **Beloved Woman**, when she was only seventeen years old.

Nanye'hi was born around 1738, and she distinguished herself very early in life. As a teenager, Nanye'hi married a Cherokee warrior named **Kingfisher** and had two children. Kingfisher fought in several wars between the Cherokee and the **Creek**, and Nanye'hi was usually at his side, loading his musket. In 1755 she and Kingfisher fought against the Creek in the **Battle of Taliwa**. During the battle, Kingfisher was shot and killed. Nanye'hi grabbed his musket and continued firing, singing a Cherokee war song. The Cherokee rallied and won the battle.

The Cherokee believed they could not have won the Battle of Taliwa without Nanye'hi and gave her the title Beloved Woman. Cherokee Beloved Women played a complementary role to that of the peace and war chiefs, who were known as Beloved Men. As a Beloved Woman, she was the leader of the women's council of clan representatives and a member of the tribal council of chiefs.

In 1776 as the American Revolution was breaking out, the Cherokee sided with the British and planned a raid on settlements in the Holston and Watauga Valleys. Nanye'hi, who now was known as **Nancy Ward**—she had married and had a child with an Irish trader named **Brian Ward** after Kingfisher's death—disapproved of the raid. She warned the settlers, and most of them escaped.

After the colonies won their independence, Nanye'hi encouraged white settlers and Cherokee chiefs to negotiate rather than fight. She traveled tirelessly between Cherokee and white communities, even though American leaders occasionally objected to negotiating with a woman. In 1785 Nanye'hi helped negotiate the **Treaty of Hopewell**, the first treaty between the Cherokee and the new United States.

However, the United States did not respect its treaties with the Cherokee Nation. In 1808 and 1817, Nanye'hi and the rest of the women's council urged the Cherokee to stop selling land to white settlers, fearing that eventually the Americans would take over all the Cherokee lands. Then the tribal council sold off Nanye'hi's home village. Forced to move, Nanye'hi opened an inn on the Ocowee River, near present-day Benton, Tennessee.

Nanye'hi died around 1822, and thus did not live to see her fears realized with the Cherokee migration west in 1835, known as the Trail of Tears. Nanye'hi is still a legend among the Cherokee, and a Chattanooga, Tennessee, chapter of the **Daughters of the American Revolution** is named after her.

JOSEPH BRANT, also known as Thayendanegea, was a Mohawk chief who persuaded many warriors of the **Iroquois Confederacy** to fight for the **British** during the American Revolutionary War. After the war, he led them to Canada, where many of their descendants still live today.

Like his sister Molly (see no. 10), Joseph Brant grew up in two worlds: one traditionally Mohawk and one British. After her marriage to William Johnson, Molly sent for her brother, and when he was nineteen, she arranged for him to attend Moor's Charity School for Indians, which later became Dartmouth College. There, he learned English so well that he became an interpreter and began translating the Bible into Mohawk. He also wrote several religious books, including a history of the Bible.

However, Brant's world was in turmoil, and he was not free to devote himself to religious studies. At the age of thirteen, he served with Molly's husband during the

French and Indian War. At age seventeen, he served with William Johnson's troops again. When he was twenty-one, Molly sent for him to come home. Brant returned to military service, this time leading a troop of Mohawk and Oneida volunteers against Pontiac (see no. 8) during Pontiac's Rebellion. After the war, Brant became an interpreter for the British Office of Indian Affairs.

In 1775 the British presented Brant with a captain's commission. He traveled to England and met King George III. When he returned, he began organizing the Iroquois to support the British during the American Revolution. He convinced most of the Mohawk, Seneca, Cayuga, and Onondaga. However, the Oneida and the Tuscarora supported the revolutionaries, and the Iroquois League was fractured for the first time in hundreds of years.

Brant's troops fought at **Cherry Valley**, **Minisink**, and the **Battle of Oriskany**, as well as others. The American revolutionaries called Brant "Monster Brant" because of his ferocity as a warrior, but they were equally ferocious, destroying approximately forty Native American villages, along with hundreds of acres of farmland.

When the war ended, Brant and many other Mohawks moved to Ontario, Canada. The British gave Brant—by then a commissioned colonel—a pension equal to half his pay, and in 1784 he arranged for Britain to grant the Iroquois some land on the Grand River in Ontario. Today, this area is known as the **Six Nations Reserve**. There, Brant raised his nine children and completed his translations of the Book of Common Prayer and the Gospel of Mark into Mohawk. Later in life, he traveled to the United States, meeting with President George Washington and speaking on behalf of peace along the American frontier.

◆ **BLACK HAWK** led the **Sauk** and **Fox** resistance to settlers who claimed their lands in the conflict that became known as the Black Hawk War.

Black Hawk was born in the Sauk summer village that later became Rock Island, Illinois. The Sauk farmed there in the summer and moved west to mine lead and hunt in the winter. Black Hawk became a warrior and, by his late teens, was leading war parties.

In 1804 southern Sauk and Mesquakie leaders signed the **Treaty of St. Louis**, turning fifty million acres of land—all tribal land east of the Mississippi, including Black Hawk's home—over to the United States.

Black Hawk believed that the leaders who signed the treaty had been intoxicated by alcohol that U.S. negotiator William Henry Harrison had offered them. Black Hawk also claimed that southern leaders could not represent the northern branches of the Sauk and Mesquakie. The leaders themselves thought that they had given the United States only the right to share their hunting grounds; however, they soon learned that the U.S. government claimed to own the land.

Along with **Tecumseh**, Black Hawk and the Sauk fought against the United States in the War of 1812. British leaders told the Native Americans that the war would not end until their land was returned to them. Instead, Britain made a peace with the United States that left the 1804 treaty in place. Black Hawk's rival, **Keokuk**, agreed to abide by the treaty, and moved a group of Mesquakie to Iowa. However, Black Hawk stayed in Illinois.

In 1829 Black Hawk and his band returned from their winter hunt to find U.S. settlers living in their lodges and plowing their fields. Shocked, the Sauk stayed, sharing their village with the settlers. In 1831 the U.S. government forced the Sauk into Iowa. They returned the next year to plant their corn as usual, knowing that this time they would have to resist the U.S. military. Black Hawk may have expected help from the British, as well as the Winnebago and the Potawatomi, but all three remained neutral.

On May 14, Black Hawk sent messengers with a flag of truce toward the U.S. troops, but nervous militiamen fired on them. The Sauk won the ensuing battle and then fled into present-day Wisconsin. Black Hawk tried to persuade his followers to march farther north, and about fifty left with him. The next day, U.S. troops massacred the remaining three hundred, including elders and children. Black Hawk was captured, imprisoned, and released the following year.

For a time, Black Hawk toured the country, telling his story. His defeat allowed the complete white settlement of what had been the Old Northwest Territory.

The **Shawnee** leader **TECUMSEH** led a confederacy of Native American nations and fought alongside the British against the United States in the **War of 1812**.

Born near present-day Springfield, Ohio, Tecumseh had a tumultuous upbringing. When he was a child, settlers began to arrive in the Ohio Valley, illegally squatting on Native American land. When he was only about six, his father was killed by settlers. A year later his mother moved to present-day Missouri, leaving Tecumseh to be raised by his sister and brother. Within a few years, **Cornstalk**, a great Shawnee leader and mentor to Tecumseh, was murdered by settlers. In years to come, Tecumseh was to see two of his brothers killed in battles against the United States.

Tecumseh came of age during the Revolutionary War, fighting with the British against the colonists. Afterward he continued to fight with settlers along the frontier, earning a reputation for treating prisoners of war humanely.

After 1790 waves of settlers moved into the Ohio Valley. During this time, some unscrupulous Native Americans sold the United States large areas of land that they did not own. Tecumseh spoke out against this practice and refused to recognize treaties such as the **Treaty of Greenville** (1795), in which Native Americans gave up their claims to south, central, and east Ohio. Tecumseh believed that land belonged collectively to all Native Americans and could not be sold by a few without the consent of all. Despite his disagreements with the United States, he sometimes agreed to negotiate on the government's behalf, speaking eloquently to calm panicky settlers and to prevent violent conflicts along the frontier.

Around 1808 Tecumseh moved to present-day Indiana and began to organize a confederacy of Native American nations. He traveled as far away as New York and Florida, rallying thousands of Native Americans to join his confederacy. However, his momentum was lost in 1811, when his brother **Tenskwatawa**—who had become a powerful Shawnee religious leader called the Prophet—ordered an attack upon **William Henry Harrison's** troops while Tecumseh was away. Harrison won the battle and destroyed the village of Tippecanoe.

In 1812, realizing that war was about to break out between the United States and Great Britain, Tecumseh and his followers—more than one thousand warriors—joined a British army in Canada. Tecumseh took command of a troop of British and Native American soldiers, earning the rank of brigadier general in the British army. In August 1812, he helped capture Detroit and 2,500 U.S. soldiers. However, by October, Britain began to suffer setbacks, and during the retreat of British troops into Canada, Tecumseh was killed at the **Battle of the Thames**. Soon after Tecumseh's death, his confederacy dissolved.

◆ **SEQUOYAH** created a system of writing for the Cherokee language that became universally adopted by the entire Cherokee Nation. He was born in Tuskegee, North Carolina, and was raised an only child by his Cherokee mother. He never attended school and never learned to read or write English. As a child, Sequoyah did not play with other children, preferring to sit by himself and draw; he had been injured on a hunting trip, and one leg was permanently disabled.

During the Creek War of 1813–1814, many Cherokee enlisted in the U.S. Army to fight their old enemy, the Creek. Sequoyah enlisted as well. In the army, Sequoyah was impressed with the usefulness of writing symbols down on paper to communicate meaning. He became determined to create a system of writing for the Cherokee.

Sequoyah worked on his project for twelve years. His family and friends thought his idea was foolish. Some Cherokee even thought Sequoyah might be practicing some form of witchcraft. More than once, they burned his work. One time they burned his entire cabin.

Sequoyah pressed on, however, finally detecting eighty-six separate sounds in the Cherokee language. To communicate these sounds, he borrowed letters from English, Greek, and Hebrew, and created some new letters himself. He also extended the Cherokee system of numbers, inventing a system of arithmetic that could express numbers up to a million. Then he taught his six-year-old daughter, **Ah-yoka**, to read and write.

In 1821 Sequoyah and Ah-yoka presented his work to the **Eastern Cherokee Tribal Council**. During the next year, Sequoyah taught thousands of Cherokee to read and write, refusing to accept payment for his teaching. The Cherokee had become the first Native American tribe north of Mexico to have its own system of writing. In 1824 the Eastern Cherokee Nation gratefully awarded Sequoyah a silver medal and a lifetime pension for his work. Then Sequoyah moved to Arkansas, where he taught his system to the **Western Cherokee**.

In 1828 the Cherokee Tribal Council began to print a newspaper using Sequoyah's system. Soon a tribal constitution was written down. Sequoyah became the president of the Western branch of the Cherokee.

In 1838 President Andrew Jackson illegally removed the Eastern Cherokee from their ancestral homeland, forcing them to march thousands of miles west to lands the government had designated "Indian Territory." Many people died of starvation, exposure, and disease during this brutal displacement. This death march, and others like it affecting other tribes of the Southeast, became known as the Trail of Tears. When the Eastern Cherokee arrived, Sequoyah helped the two branches of Cherokee to work together to create one government for the Cherokee Nation.

Some Native American leaders resisted the westward expansion of the United States by putting up a physical fight. Others found nonviolent methods of resistance. **KENNEKUK**, the leader of the Vermillion (the northern) branch of the **Kickapoo**, was one such person.

Traditionally, the Kickapoo were a wandering, hunter-gatherer people. As the United States expanded westward, the government encouraged Native Americans to become farmers; of course, many Native American economies were already based on farming. Kennekuk knew that white settlers would feel less threatened by a community of Native Americans who were peaceful farmers. Hoping that the Kickapoo would be able to coexist with the settlers and keep their land, he encouraged his followers to take up farming. They did, and the U.S. government helped subsidize the farms that he established.

Kennekuk was not just a political leader but a religious one too. At the same time he pushed the Kickapoo to transform their economy, he also taught his followers to adhere to their traditional religious beliefs. After experiencing an intense religious vision, Kennekuk taught the Kickapoo to fast and meditate regularly. He also spoke out against violent behavior and the consumption of alcohol.

Kennekuk's strategy for keeping Kickapoo lands worked, but only for a while. The Kickapoo prospered as farmers, and settlers coveted their fields. During the 1820s, the famous explorer **William Clark**, who was then Superintendent of Indian Affairs in St. Louis, met often with Kennekuk, urging him to sign a treaty to give up the land and agree to move elsewhere.

At first Kennekuk refused. Then he began to use passive resistance to delay the relocation of his people. He met frequently with government officials, telling them that the Kickapoo had decided to move but were not ready yet. He offered a variety of excuses, such as the harvest or illness in the community, for the delays. In this way he was able to postpone the move for more than ten years.

After the **Black Hawk War** of 1832 (see no. 13), settlers were nervous about living so close to a Native American community, even a peaceful one. The government finally forced Kennekuk to sign a treaty agreeing to relocate to Kansas. Even after signing the treaty, Kennekuk managed to delay the move, but he and his band finally relocated in 1833.

In the years that followed, Kennekuk continued to use his skills as a shrewd negotiator to benefit the Kickapoo. He also continued to teach his traditional religion. Kennekuk caught smallpox and died in 1852, just as the government began pressuring the Kickapoo to give up more land. His band of the Kickapoo grew smaller, until eventually its last members died.

◆ **SACAJAWEA** served as a guide and interpreter for American explorers **Meriwether Lewis** and **William Clark** on their historic journey to explore the newly acquired territory of the **Louisiana Purchase** in the early 1800s.

Many specific details of Sacajawea's life are unknown. A member of the **Shoshone**, she was probably born in the late 1780s in present-day central Idaho. When Sacajawea was about twelve, **Hidatsa** warriors attacked her family's camp, killing eight adults and kidnapping Sacajawea and several other children. Between 1800 and 1804, Sacajawea and another girl were either sold to or won in a gambling match by a French-Canadian trader named **Toussaint Charbonneau**. Later, Charbonneau married both girls.

In October of 1804, Lewis and Clark's expedition arrived at Sacajawea's village in present-day **North Dakota**. The explorers built cabins and decided to stay for the winter. When he learned about the expedition, Charbonneau offered the services of himself and Sacajawea as interpreters for their trip. Lewis and Clark accepted the offer, though Sacajawea was pregnant. She gave birth to a son, **Jean-Baptiste**, in February, and carried him on her back in a cradleboard when the expedition headed west in the spring.

The lone female member of the forty-man expedition, Sacajawea made invaluable contributions on the journey west. She interpreted for the explorers as they encountered various tribes, as well as provided expert guidance through present-day Montana. She also gathered edible plants for everyone to eat, and on one occasion, she saved their journals, instruments, and medicine after Charbonneau accidentally capsized one of the boats.

In midsummer, the party entered Shoshone territory, where Sacajawea was reunited with her brother, who had become the Shoshone leader. At her request, he provided horses, supplies, and guides to help the explorers make their way across the Rocky Mountains. After navigating the Clearwater, Snake, and Columbia Rivers, the party reached the Pacific Ocean in November 1805.

When the expedition returned to Sacajawea's village in 1806, Clark offered to adopt her son, Jean-Baptiste. Charbonneau and Sacajawea refused the offer, but sometime later they traveled to St. Louis to leave him with Clark to receive a Western education. Clark later adopted Jean-Baptiste as his own, believing that Sacajawea was dead.

Historians, however, are uncertain when Sacajawea died. Some believe, as Clark did, that she died at age twenty-five of a fever. Others believe that it was Charbonneau's other wife who died of the fever. Shoshone oral tradition claims that Sacajawea married a Comanche man, had five more children, became an important political leader, and lived to be one hundred. In addition to numerous memorials along the explorers' route, Sacajawea also has a river, a mountain, and a pass named in her honor.

18 SEATHL

c. 1790–1866

SEATHL, the leader for whom the city of **Seattle** is named, is often regarded as the last great Native American leader of the Pacific Northwest.

The principal chief of the **Duwamish, Suquamish**, and allied nations, Seathl was born near Puget Sound around 1788. He was about four years old when English navigator **George Vancouver** sailed into the sound, hoping to find a route through the continent to Hudson Bay, and met with the Duwamish and Suquamish. However, after Vancouver's visit, these Native Americans saw very few settlers from the United States and Canada for the next several decades.

During his early years, Seathl became a warrior, and was respected for his fearlessness in battle. Meanwhile, more settlers moved west toward the Pacific. In 1833 the **Hudson's Bay Company** built a trading post at the southern end of Puget Sound. During the 1830s, Catholic missionaries traveled to the region and converted Seathl to **Christianity.** From that time on, historians believe, Seathl was determined to coexist peacefully with the settlers he knew would eventually be on their way. It wasn't until the early 1850s, however, that the first settlers arrived to establish what would later become the city of Seattle.

When they did arrive, the Duwamish and Suquamish welcomed and helped them. The settlers wanted to honor Seathl for his help by naming their community "Seattle." The chief objected to this on the grounds that after he was dead, his spirit would be disturbed if people said his name. Eventually, he persuaded settlers to pay him a small tax to compensate him in advance for the disturbance to his spirit.

Although the Duwamish and Suquamish remained at peace with the settlers, other Pacific Northwest nations rebelled against the encroachments on their land. In 1855 territorial governor **Isaac Stevens** asked some nations to move onto reservations. Seathl and other leaders agreed, after insisting that some of their most-prized lands be included as part of the reservations. Seathl was the first to sign the **Port Elliott Treaty**, stipulating the boundaries of the reservations. Then he gave an eloquent farewell address. Since at least four versions of the speech survive today, nobody is sure exactly what Seathl said, although he is often quoted. In one version, Seathl remarks, "How can you buy or sell the sky, the warmth of the land? The idea is strange to us."

Several Native American nations in the Pacific Northwest refused to accept the Port Elliott Treaty, and battles continued for more than fifteen years. Seathl, however, refused to allow his community to go to war, and ensured that his people lived in peace and safety on the reservation he had chosen for them.

Many historians consider **MANGAS COLORADAS** to be the most important **Apache** leader of the nineteenth century, because he united the Apache nation against the United States.

Mangas's band lived in the Mimbres Mountains, in southern **New Mexico**, which was at the time part of Mexico, a colony of Spain. While historically the Apache had considered Mexico their enemy, during Mangas Coloradas's youth, the two sides were at peace. They went to war again after Mexico won its independence from Spain in 1821. By 1835, Apache warriors had killed five thousand Mexican settlers. The Mexican states then placed a bounty on all Apache scalps.

A special bounty was placed on the head of the Mimbreño Apache leader, **Juan Jose Compas**. In 1837 an Anglo American trapper whom Compas trusted as a friend arrived at Compas's camp with a band of armed men and killed him and twenty other Apaches to obtain the reward money. After Compas's death, Mangas Coloradas became the leader of the **Mimbreño**. He began a series of retaliatory raids that would eventually make his name, as one historian has remarked, "synonymous with terror."

Yet Mangas also tried to bring about peace, sometimes risking his own life to do so. In 1846 he signed a peace treaty with the United States, which had taken possession of New Mexico after the Mexican War, and provided troops with safe passage through Apache territory. However, in 1851, Anglo gold miners arrived in the Santa Rita Mountains, angering the Apache. Mangas approached the miners and offered to lead them to another area. The miners tied him to a tree and whipped him severely, saying that this was a warning "for Indians to stay away from whites."

In revenge, Mangas raided local settlements. In 1852 he and other leaders signed a peace treaty at Acoma, but the treaty was not ratified by Congress, and the raids continued. The situation grew so bad that a U.S. Army report recommended giving New Mexico back to the Native Americans and to Mexico.

Mangas Coloradas arranged alliances between his band and several others. He and another Apache leader, **Cochise** (see no. 26), became allies in 1861. They tried to drive all Anglo Americans out of Apache territory. They nearly succeeded, reducing the Anglo population of New Mexico and Arizona for several years.

In 1863 U.S. soldiers invited Mangas to negotiate a peace. He rode alone to **Fort McClean**, where he was captured. Brigadier General **J. R. West** told soldiers that he didn't want Mangas to be alive the next morning. The soldiers tortured and killed him, later claiming he had been killed while trying to escape.

BLACK KETTLE, a leader of the **Southern Cheyenne**, struggled—unsuccessfully—to bring about peace between his community and the U.S. government at a time when tensions between settlers and Native Americans were extremely high.

As a young man, Black Kettle participated in wars against the **Ute** and **Delaware**. However, he advocated peace with the United States. In 1851 the Cheyenne signed the **Treaty of Fort Laramie**, which guaranteed them lands in western Kansas and eastern Colorado. During the 1859 gold rush, though, settlers rushed into the area in violation of the treaty.

In 1861 Black Kettle signed a treaty agreeing to a reservation at **Sand Creek**, Colorado, although the land there was not farmable, and the nearest buffalo herd was two hundred miles away. Black Kettle could not stop young Cheyenne warriors from raiding settlements and wagon trains, and state militias did not distinguish between peaceful and hostile Native Americans. Settlers were terrified, and newspapers called for the extermination of all Native Americans. Black Kettle visited **Fort Weld**, Colorado, to negotiate for peace and received permission to camp at Sand Creek during the negotiations.

However, Colorado's governor had formed citizen militias who were authorized to kill any hostile Native Americans they could find. One militia, armed with howitzer cannons and led by Colonel **John Chivington**, approached Black Kettle's camp at dawn, November 29, 1864. Of the six hundred people in the camp, only about thirty-five were warriors; the rest were old men, women, and children.

Black Kettle raised the U.S. flag and a white flag to show his peaceful intentions, and junior officers riding with Chivington told him that these Cheyenne had given up their weapons and been promised army protection. Nevertheless, Chivington ordered his troops to attack. About two hundred Cheyenne, mostly women and children, were killed and their bodies mutilated.

Despite the massacre, Black Kettle continued to press for peace. He signed treaties in 1865 and 1867 and led his community to reservations first in Kansas and then in Oklahoma. He kept the peace, although some Cheyenne bands continued to make war. When fighting broke out in the fall of 1868, Black Kettle visited **Fort Cobb** to tell the commander that he wanted peace. Told that the only safe place for his people was the area around the fort, Black Kettle began preparing to move.

On the day his band was to leave, Colonel **George Custer** and the Seventh Cavalry attacked his camp, although it was flying a white flag. They killed Black Kettle and more than one hundred others, ninety-three of whom were old men, women, and children.

OSCEOLA led the **Seminole** resistance to the U.S. government's plan to relocate eastern Native American nations to lands west of the Mississippi River during the 1830s.

The Seminole are a nation originally made up of Creek who migrated to **Florida** from Georgia, their African American slaves, fugitive slaves, and their descendants. Osceola himself was born in Georgia. After the Creek War, a civil war between two factions of Creek, Osceola and his mother moved to Florida.

In 1819 Spain sold Florida to the United States, and in 1823 the U.S. government moved the Seminole to a Florida reservation. The land on the reservation was poor, but the Seminole lived there peacefully. Osceola worked as a guide and helped surveyors mark reservation boundaries. After a few years, the Seminole asked for a grant of swampland, and Osceola moved to the Everglades.

In 1830 Congress passed the **Indian Removal Act**, authorizing President **Andrew Jackson** to offer eastern Native American nations lands west of the Mississippi River. The **Chickasaw**, **Choctaw**, **Seminole**, **Cherokee**, and **Creek** resisted the move, and Jackson decided to use the military to evict them. As many as 25 percent of some groups died on these forced marches.

In 1832 the government decided to move the Seminole to **Arkansas** and reunite them with the Creek, who many Seminole had fought during the Creek War. A few Seminole leaders signed a treaty agreeing to this, but others were horrified, especially because the treaty required that Seminole of African American descent be treated as runaway slaves. Osceola knew what it was like to lose a loved one to slave catchers—his wife, the daughter of a fugitive slave, had been seized and shipped to the slave states. He began organizing resistance to the relocation.

In 1835 U.S. agent **Wiley Thompson** tried to force a new removal and relocation treaty on the Seminole. Most Seminole leaders refused to sign it, and Osceola slashed the treaty with his knife. Thompson imprisoned Osceola, who finally signed the treaty in order to be released. Then he vanished into the Everglades, where many Seminole took their families to hide.

For two years Osceola and his followers waged a guerrilla war against the United States. While the Seminole were outnumbered, they managed to kill hundreds of U.S. soldiers. In 1837 Osceola met General **Thomas Jesup** under a truce flag. However, Jesup arrested him. Osceola died of unknown causes in prison in 1838.

The Seminole continued to resist relocation, led by **Billy Bowlegs** (see no. 24) among others, but over the next five years, approximately 3,800 Seminole were removed to Arkansas. A few hundred remained in the Everglades.

WASHAKIE was an **Eastern Shoshoni** leader who befriended **Oregon Trail settlers** and the U.S. Army during the mid-1800s. His insistence on peaceful coexistence with settlers helped him bargain for a reservation on fertile land in traditional Shoshoni territory, present-day western Wyoming.

As a young man, Washakie earned a reputation as a courageous warrior, fighting in battles against the **Blackfeet** and **Crow**. Throughout his life, he continued to fight Native American enemies of the Shoshoni while remaining at peace with the United States.

During the 1820s and 1830s, Washakie befriended the explorers, trappers, and traders who arrived in his territory. He became the principal leader of his community in the 1840s, when settlers were beginning to migrate along the Oregon Trail. He refused to allow Shoshoni warriors to harm the settlers, even when settlers destroyed herds and lands that the Shoshoni needed.

Instead, Washakie provided Shoshoni warrior patrols to protect the immigrants from raids by the **Sioux**, **Cheyenne**, and **Arapaho**, enemies of the Shoshoni. He also helped settlers find lost cattle and cross rivers safely. Nine thousand settlers signed a document commending Washakie and thanking him for his help.

In 1862, against Washakie's orders, a group of Shoshoni joined the Bannock in raiding some emigrant wagon trains and settlements. Knowing there was a danger that settlers would try to punish his entire community for these acts, Washakie led the Eastern Shoshoni to take refuge at Fort Bridger. They were reunited with the rest of the Shoshoni in 1863. That year, Washakie signed a treaty guaranteeing safe passage to travelers.

In 1868 he agreed to settle the Eastern Shoshoni on the **Wind River Reservation**. Washakie did not want to confine his people to a reservation. However, he made a practical decision, ensuring that his community would be able to remain in its homeland, safe from the massacres that were being suffered by so many other Native American nations.

Younger warriors sometimes criticized Washakie's cooperation with the U.S. government. When the government violated its treaty with the Shoshoni in 1870, reducing the amount of land set aside for the reservation, some young warriors tried to remove Washakie as chief. Washakie, who was nearly seventy, left camp, returning two months later with six scalps of Native American enemies of the Shoshoni. His critics stopped complaining.

Throughout the rest of his life, Washakie continued to help the army, providing scouts to help the U.S. government in its wars against the Arapaho, Cheyenne, Sioux, and Ute. When he died in 1900, Washakie was buried with full military honors at a fort the army named after him.

STAND WATIE signed the treaty that authorized removal of the **Cherokee** nation to Oklahoma, and later became a brigadier general in the **Confederate army** during the Civil War.

Watie was born in Georgia and educated at mission schools. When he returned home from school, he became a planter and also helped publish the *Cherokee Phoenix* newspaper. At the time, the Cherokee nation was divided on the question of what to do about settlers taking their lands. Watie became a member of the **Treaty Party** which advocated signing a treaty to give up land in Georgia in exchange for land in the west.

Although not authorized to do so, Watie and other members of his party signed a treaty agreeing to the removal of the Cherokee to Oklahoma. The lawful government of the Cherokee petitioned the U.S. Senate not to ratify the treaty, and after it did so anyway, contested the removal plans in the Supreme Court. The Cherokee won their case, but President **Andrew Jackson** illegally decided to force them to move anyway.

In the meantime, Watie and his family had already moved to Oklahoma, along with other members of the Treaty Party. Watie brought with him the slaves from his plantation and established a new plantation at his new home. The rest of the Cherokee were forced to march the infamous **Trail of Tears** during the winter of 1838–1839, and thousands died along the way because of hunger, cold, and exhaustion.

When the Eastern Cherokee arrived, they vigorously disagreed with the Western Cherokee—those Cherokee who, like Watie, had already moved west—about the form their new government should take. All the Cherokee who had signed the treaty were killed, except for Watie, who was warned and managed to escape. Over time, however, the Cherokee settled their differences. Watie served as a member of the **Cherokee National Council** for more than a decade and was its speaker for two years.

When the Civil War began, many Cherokee supported the Confederacy. Some Cherokee owned slaves, and many wanted revenge against the Union for the Trail of Tears. Other Cherokee fought on the side of the Union. Watie organized a Cherokee regiment and was commissioned as a colonel in the Confederate army. In 1864 he was promoted to brigadier general, the only Native American to hold that rank in either army during the Civil War. After the war, Stand Watie helped negotiate the 1866 Cherokee Reconstruction Treaty. He died in 1871.

BILLY BOWLEGS led the **Seminole** resistance to relocation in the **Second** and **Third Seminole Wars**. Bowlegs's band became one of the last bands to stay in **Florida** after the U.S. government began trying to relocate them.

Bowlegs was only eight years old at the time of the First Seminole War. He became a chief of the Seminole at the age of twenty, in time to lead a group of guerrillas in the Second Seminole War (1835–1842). Bowlegs fought alongside **Osceola** (see no. 21) until he was captured. Like Osceola, several Seminole leaders were captured under truce flags and taken to **Arkansas**. When these leaders were kidnapped, their followers began to surrender and move west.

By the end of the Second Seminole War, only a few hundred Seminole remained in Florida. Billy Bowlegs and his followers were among them. Bowlegs agreed to a treaty that allotted some land in Florida to the remaining Seminole. However, at the same time, the U.S. government continued to negotiate with Bowlegs about the possibility of relocating the rest of the Seminole community westward. Bowlegs did everything he could to prolong the negotiations, knowing that his people could live in peace while the matter was pending.

In 1852 Bowlegs and other Seminole leaders met with President **Millard Fillmore** in Washington, DC. The army hoped the trip would convince the Seminole leaders that the United States was too powerful to be resisted, but Bowlegs was determined not to leave his home.

In 1855 a group of army engineers and surveyors trampled some Seminole farmland, destroying crops and taking produce. Some historians believe the engineers were provoking Bowlegs on purpose to see what he would do. As a result, he took up arms

again, starting the Third Seminole War (1855–1858).

Bowlegs and his followers fought on, long after most of the remaining Seminole had surrendered and moved west. As he and his band grew short of supplies, the army sent a group of Arkansas Seminole to persuade him to migrate west. Bowlegs agreed, but some of his followers did not. They remained in Florida, living in isolated parts of the **Everglades**. Today their descendants are proud to say they are the only Native American nation never to surrender to the United States.

Billy Bowlegs traveled to the Seminole reservation; however, beyond that, historians are not quite sure what became of him. Some believe he died of smallpox in 1859 or 1864, while others claim he fought as a Union soldier in the Civil War and died in 1861.

DULL KNIFE was the coleader of the **Northern Cheyenne** on their 1,500-mile journey from their reservation in Oklahoma back to their homeland in Montana. The Cheyenne who survived the journey received a reservation in **Montana's Rosebud Valley**.

Dull Knife's actual name was **Morning Star**, but most people called him Dull Knife because his brother-in-law liked to joke that his knife was not sharp. As a young man, Dull Knife earned a reputation as a warrior and became a member of his tribal government. By the time he was in his sixties, he had become one of four chiefs who, according to Cheyenne tradition, stood for four Sacred Persons who lived at the universe's cardinal points and guarded creation.

Dull Knife joined **Red Cloud's** band (see no. 29) in Red Cloud's War in 1866, and may have helped **Crazy Horse** (see no. 41) defeat Colonel **George Custer** at the **Battle of the Little Bighorn**. In 1876 an army force looking for Crazy Horse found Dull Knife's camp instead, and a battle ensued. During the battle, the entire camp—including shelters, clothing, blankets, and food—was destroyed. The survivors fled to Crazy Horse's camp, and eleven children froze to death on the journey.

With Crazy Horse, Dull Knife decided to surrender, and his community moved to a reservation in Oklahoma. The land was not suitable for farming or hunting, and there were malaria epidemics. Half the Cheyenne died in the first year. Dull Knife and another Cheyenne chief, **Little Wolf** (see no. 28), asked to be relocated to the Plains, but the army refused. In September 1878, Dull Knife and Little Wolf led a group of three hundred off the reservation and headed home, with ten thousand soldiers on their trail. In Nebraska, the two leaders split up.

Dull Knife's band was captured and taken to **Fort Robinson**; after refusing to return to Oklahoma, they were jailed in a freezing barracks with no food or water for three days. Finally they tried to escape, making a run for it with their children under their arms and on their backs. Soldiers shot at them as they fled, killing twenty-two men, eight women, and two children. Most of the others were recaptured, but a few, including Dull Knife and some of his family members, escaped. They spent eighteen days walking to the **Pine Ridge Reservation** in South Dakota, subsisting on bark.

At this point, the government abandoned its efforts to relocate the Northern Cheyenne to Oklahoma and gave the surviving members of both Dull Knife's and Little Wolf's bands a reservation in their home territory in Montana. Dull Knife died there around 1883.

COCHISE, a leader of the **Chiricahua Apache**, led his people's resistance to white settlement of the Southwest during the 1860s. A formidable warrior, he later became such a force for peace that when he became deathly ill, even Anglo settlers feared the possible consequences of his demise.

Historians know very little about Cochise's early life. They do know that as a young man, at times he helped American settlers. In 1858 Cochise agreed to guard stagecoaches passing through Apache territory. He was regarded throughout the region as a peaceful, fair, honorable person. However, in 1861 army lieutenant **George Bascom** wrongly accused him of having kidnapped an Anglo child and tried to arrest him. Cochise cut a hole in the side of his tent and escaped, despite being shot three times. Bascom did arrest six other Apache warriors, so Cochise kidnapped three Anglos and attempted to organize a prisoner exchange. Bascom refused, and they both killed their prisoners.

Cochise joined forces with **Mangas Coloradas** (see no. 19). Together, they drove Anglos out of **New Mexico** and **Arizona** during the Civil War. After Mangas died in 1863, Cochise and his band so terrorized Anglo settlements that General **William Tecumseh Sherman** remarked that the United States had fought one war with Mexico to get the Southwest, and should fight another "to make her take it back."

Despite Cochise's reputation for cruelty during war, Anglos who approached his camp peacefully could be received peacefully. In 1871 the army changed its approach to the Apache wars, sending out scouts to locate individual bands of Apache and negotiate peace with them, instead of trying to conquer them.

Meanwhile, a mail carrier named **Thomas Jeffords**, who had lost fourteen employees to Cochise's warriors, decided to pay Cochise a visit. He walked up to Cochise's camp alone, and offered his firearms in exchange for a talk. The two negotiated a deal, and from then on, Jeffords's mail carriers were allowed to pass safely through Cochise's territory.

Jeffords also arranged a meeting between Cochise and General **Oliver Howard** in 1872, and Howard offered Cochise a reservation in New Mexico. He considered the offer, but warned Howard that many Apache would not be willing to go there. Instead, he promised General Howard that the Chiricahua Apache would stop fighting in return for a reservation in the Chiricahua Mountains. He kept that promise all his life.

Unfortunately, the army, not realizing that Cochise could not speak for all the Apache, blamed him when some Apache continued to wage war. The U.S. government then decided to shut down the Chiricahua reservation and send the Apache to New Mexico, but Cochise died before that occurred.

MANUELITO was a major **Navajo** war leader. After the Navajo made their tragic **Long Walk**, Manuelito helped persuade the government that they should have a reservation in their homeland.

In 1848 the United States ended its war with Mexico and annexed the Southwest as a new U.S. territory. In 1855, the same year that Manuelito became a chief in his community, the U.S. government built **Fort Defiance**, in present-day **New Mexico**, near an area the Navajo used as grazing land for their horses.

The post commander decided to use the area adjacent to the fort as grazing land for the fort's horses, and ordered the Navajo to move their livestock. Manuelito defiantly refused, and one day the army shot sixty of his horses and more than one hundred sheep. The situation escalated until the Navajo attacked Fort Defiance. However, the war lasted only a few weeks before a peace treaty was signed.

In 1861, however, troops began to leave the area to fight in the Civil War. Navajo chiefs Manuelito, **Barboncito**, and **Herrero Grande** saw a chance to drive the remaining soldiers away, and they persuaded between one and two thousand Navajo, **Ute**, **Apache**, and **Pueblo** to join them in attacking the fort. However, the fort's commander had been warned of the surprise attack, and the soldiers managed to drive the warriors back with cannons.

In 1863 General **James Carleton** began a massive effort to force the Navajo to relocate to **Bosque Redondo**, a reservation in New Mexico. He assigned Colonel **Kit Carson** to do the job. Knowing he could not defeat the Navajo militarily in their homeland, Carson began destroying Navajo homes, crops, and livestock. Forced to subsist on berries and wild nuts, they could not make it through the winter.

In February 1864, they began turning themselves in, to begin what became known as the Long Walk. More than two hundred Navajo died during this 350-mile journey. Some died of hunger and cold, and others drowned in the Rio Grande, which they were forced to cross during the spring flood. When they arrived at Bosque Redondo, conditions were no better. More than two thousand Navajo died there of disease and starvation. The army removed General Carleton from command, and in 1868 Manuelito and other chiefs traveled to Washington, DC, to negotiate for their return home.

Although the government had planned to relocate the Navajo to Oklahoma, Manuelito pleaded eloquently for the Navajo to return to their homeland. Finally, the government agreed to a 3.5-million-acre reservation in the Southwest.

From 1870 to 1885, Manuelito served as the principal chief of the Navajo nation. During his tenure, the Navajo rebuilt their communities, and many Navajo became prosperous ranchers.

As a strong advocate of peace and cooperation with the U.S. government, **LITTLE WOLF** helped the **Northern Cheyenne** survive an arduous journey from their Oklahoma reservation back to their Montana homeland.

As a teenager, Little Wolf became known as a warrior. However, as American settlers began to arrive in the Cheyenne native lands, Little Wolf advocated living peacefully with them. He broke the peace only once, attacking army troops in 1865 to avenge their 1864 massacre of Cheyenne at **Sand Creek**. Like **Dull Knife** (see no. 25), **Little Wolf** and his followers were attacked following the **Battle of the Little Bighorn**; to avoid a bloodbath, they surrendered and moved to the Cheyenne reservation in Oklahoma.

On the reservation, there was little food, and half the band died of malaria and pneumonia. Dull Knife and Little Wolf asked to be relocated to Montana, but U.S. agent **John Miles** suggested that they wait a year. Little Wolf replied that the Cheyenne would be dead in a year. A few weeks later, Miles angrily confronted Little Wolf when several Cheyenne ran away from the reservation, demanding hostages against their return. Little Wolf refused, and Miles threatened to withhold rations. Little Wolf replied, "Last night I saw children eating grass because they had no food. Will you take the grass from them?"

As a leader of the Northern Cheyenne, Little Wolf carried their chief's Sacred Bundle, which meant that he was considered to be personally responsible for their welfare. So Little Wolf and Dull Knife led their communities away from the reservation. Little Wolf planned the strategy that helped them evade the ten thousand soldiers who pursued them.

In Nebraska, he and Dull Knife separated. Several regiments of soldiers followed Little Wolf, but when his band saw soldiers, he always insisted that the Cheyenne should not be the first ones to shoot. Finally, one troop caught up with Little Wolf and persuaded him to surrender and come to **Fort Keogh**.

At Fort Keogh, the commanding general promised the Cheyenne a reservation in their home territory. Eventually, they were reunited with Dull Knife on the reservation in **Montana's Rosebud Valley**, having suffered far fewer casualties than Dull Knife's band.

Confinement on a reservation, even in their home territory, however, was difficult. Little Wolf and several of his warriors enlisted in the army as Indian scouts, a well-paying job that allowed them more freedom than they had on the reservation. Little Wolf lived for another thirty years and died at the age of eighty-four.

RED CLOUD was a leader of the **Oglala Lakota**, the largest group of the **Sioux** nation. He was the first Native American leader in the West to win a war against the United States—and the last.

Red Cloud earned the respect of his community in his youth, as a warrior against the Pawnee, the Crow, the Ute, and the Shoshoni. Until 1865, though, the Oglala remained at peace with settlers traveling through their territory. Then gold was discovered in **Montana**, and the U.S. government tried to develop the **Bozeman Trail** for miners to travel on, building forts to protect the miners in the heart of Lakota hunting grounds. Red Cloud led the Plains nations to war, besieging one fort and cutting off its food supplies, and effectively closing the wagon road.

In 1866 the government tried to negotiate for peace. The negotiations, held at Fort Laramie, looked promising until seven hundred troops arrived, expecting to erect

a chain of forts along the Bozeman Trail. Furious, Red Cloud stormed out, accusing the peace commissioners of planning to take the country by force whether or not Native Americans signed the treaty.

Red Cloud began attacking troops traveling on the Bozeman Trail, and in one case, his warriors ambushed a regiment of soldiers, leaving no survivors. It became impossible to use the Bozeman Trail. When the government planned another peace conference in 1867, Red Cloud sent a message: "When we see the soldiers moving away and the forts abandoned, then I will come down and talk."

In 1868 the U.S. Department of War finally evacuated the forts, which the Lakota and the **Cheyenne** burned to the ground. A few weeks later, Red Cloud signed a peace treaty. He had fought for several years to preserve his people's hunting grounds. Now the soldiers were gone, the forts were destroyed, and the Bozeman Trail was closed. Red Cloud had won his war.

The treaty guaranteed western South Dakota, including the **Black Hills**, and much of Montana and Wyoming, to the Lakota. Red Cloud laid down his arms, and settled on a Nebraska reservation.

The United States abided by its treaty for just a few years, until gold was discovered in the Black Hills. When the Lakota refused to sell the Black Hills, the United States went to war against them. However, Red Cloud had promised never to make war again, and during the war of 1876–1877, he kept his word.

In 1878 he moved to the **Pine Ridge Reservation**. He spent his remaining years using peaceful methods to try to help his community, making several trips to Washington, DC, to press the government to keep the promises it made in its treaties.

◆ **VICTORIO**, the successor to **Mangas Coloradas** (see no. 19) as leader of the **Mimbreño Apache**, had a desire to live in peace with Anglo settlers. Several times he led his band to reservations, only to leave again when conditions proved to be intolerable.

Victorio eluded the U.S. and Mexican armies so often that one army official called him the "greatest Indian general who had ever appeared on the American continent."

As a young man, Victorio fought alongside Mangas Coloradas against Mexico and the United States. When Mangas was killed, Victorio became the leader of the Mimbreño band who were living at Ojo Caliente (Warm Springs). He fought Mexico and the United States for several years, while also working to negotiate a peace.

In 1870 the Mimbreño agreed to live on what was supposed to be a permanent reservation in their home territory in southwest New Mexico. In the spring of 1877, however, the U.S. government ordered Victorio's band to move to the **San Carlos Reservation** in southeast Arizona to live with other Apache groups, some of whom were their enemies. Victorio hid a stockpile of weapons and led his band to San Carlos to attempt to live in their new home.

By the fall of 1877, the Mimbreño were miserable in the hot, overcrowded reservation that one army officer called "Hell's Forty Acres." With three hundred Mimbreño, Victorio left the reservation. Using a combination of raids and diplomacy, he convinced officials to allow the Mimbreño to again settle at Ojo Caliente. The army agreed but then decided to relocate them to the **Mescalero Reservation**. Victorio at first resisted this move but then agreed to it. In 1879, however, Victorio was indicted on an old charge of murder and horse-stealing. He fled the reservation with a group of Mimbreño and Mescalero.

For more than a year, Victorio and his band lived as fugitives, moving back and forth between the United States and Mexico while being pursued by the armies of both countries. During that time, they somehow managed to remain in close contact with their friends and relatives on the Mescalero Reservation. Victorio's ability to avoid capture was especially remarkable because he and his warriors usually traveled with their families, including old people and children.

In 1880 the **Mexican Army** trapped Victorio and his followers in the Tres Castillos Mountains. After two days of fighting, Victorio is said to have stabbed himself to death rather than accept captivity. Nearly eighty Mimbreño were killed in the battle, and the rest were captured.

BIG FOOT was the leader of the band of Sioux who were massacred at **Wounded Knee Creek**, South Dakota, in 1890.

As a young man, Big Foot was regarded as a skillful negotiator. He often settled quarrels between rival groups and used diplomacy to avoid war whenever possible. He became the leader of the **Miniconjou Sioux** when his father died in 1874. Big Foot allied himself with **Sitting Bull** (see no. 35) and **Crazy Horse** (see no. 41) during the war of 1876–1877 but did not play a major role in the fighting.

After the war, Big Foot settled on the **Cheyenne River Reservation** and became one of the first Sioux to raise a corn crop there. He advised his community to retain their traditions while shifting to a farming economy. He also traveled to Washington, DC, and lobbied for a school to be built on the reservation.

By 1890 conditions on the Plains reservations had reached their lowest point. The government had continued to take reservation land, and many Sioux were on the verge of starving because of the reduction of their hunting grounds. Corrupt agents often took money the government had earmarked for food and supplies for the reservations. In addition, government officials tried to eradicate Native American culture by making their traditional clothing and religions illegal.

During this difficult time, many Sioux turned to a religion founded by **Wovoka**, a Paiute mystic. Wovoka preached that Native Americans could restore their old world by renouncing war and violence, praying to the Great Spirit, and performing a special dance and chanting. This would cause dead Native Americans to be resurrected, the buffalo to return, and white settlers to leave. Many of Big Foot's followers embraced this religion, which the whites called the **Ghost Dance religion**.

As the movement spread, the United States banned the religion and sent Lakota police to bring in Sitting Bull, who the government feared might lead a mass Indian uprising. He was killed during his arrest. Some Sioux leaders decided to bring their communities to the reservation headquarters for their own safety, and Big Foot was considering this, when troops arrived and arrested them. The Miniconjou had heard how Sitting Bull had died, and they fled, but soldiers recaptured them and escorted them to Wounded Knee Creek.

Soldiers began to disarm the Miniconjou. Somewhere, a gun went off, and the **Seventh Cavalry** began to fire on them. When it was over, more than two hundred Miniconjou were dead, including Big Foot; two-thirds of those killed were women and children. The Battle of Wounded Knee Creek was the final battle of the Plains Wars in the American West.

◆ **ELY SAMUEL PARKER**, the first Native American to be **Commissioner of Indian Affairs** for the U.S. government, was born on the Tonawanda Reservation in New York State. He was the grandson of **Handsome Lake** (see no. 9) and the son of a **Seneca** chief.

Like many Native Americans of his generation, Parker began his education at a mission boarding school. Later he attended private academies. As a teenager, he was such an able interpreter that he served as a translator for Seneca delegations to Washington, DC. While still in his teens, Parker helped ethnologist **Lewis Henry Morgan** prepare a famous ethnography of the Iroquois. In his early twenties, Parker was honored with the title of "Keeper of the Western Door," an important office in the Iroquois Confederacy.

Parker originally hoped to become a lawyer, and he studied for and passed the bar exam. However, New York refused to admit him to the bar, because Native Americans were not recognized as U.S. citizens. So Parker decided to become a civil engineer. He attended **Rensselaer Polytechnic Institute**, and became a successful engineer, working on the **Erie Canal** and other public works.

When the Civil War began, Parker tried to enlist on the Union side, but Secretary of State William Seward told him that "the whites would win the war without Indian help." In 1863 Parker managed to obtain a commission as a captain of engineers, and later became the military secretary for an old friend of his, General **Ulysses S. Grant**. When Confederate general Robert E. Lee surrendered at Appomattox Court House in 1865, it was Parker who penned the official copies of the terms of surrender. Over the next several years, Parker continued to serve in the army, working his way up to the rank of brigadier general.

After Grant was elected president, he appointed Parker the first Native American to be Commissioner of Indian Affairs. In that position, he worked to reform and restructure the office and helped generate public outrage over the army's treatment of the Plains nations during the Plains Wars.

Parker made many enemies as commissioner, and eventually they accused him of defrauding the government; he was tried and found not guilty in the Congress. Parker resigned his position anyway, and went on to make and lose a fortune in the stock market. He became the superintendent of buildings for the New York City Police Department, and held that position until he died in 1895.

STANDING BEAR was a chief of the **Ponca**, a small nation related to the **Omaha**. He became famous when he sued the U.S. Army and won his case after the Ponca were forcibly moved to Oklahoma.

A small nation of between eight hundred and nine hundred people, the Ponca worked hard to maintain peace with the United States. In 1858 they gave up all their land except the area around the Niobrara River in **Nebraska**, which was guaranteed by treaty as their permanent home. Then in 1868, the United States accidentally awarded the Ponca's land to the **Sioux**, and the Sioux began trying to drive the Ponca off the land. In 1875 the government admitted it had made a mistake and proposed that the Ponca move to **Oklahoma**.

In 1877 agents of the Commissioner of Indian Affairs escorted Standing Bear and several other Ponca leaders to Oklahoma so they could pick a location for their new reservation. However, the Ponca leaders found all the suggested sites uninhabitable, and refused to relocate. The agents told them that if they wanted to return home, they would have to walk, so they did—all five hundred miles.

When they finally arrived, some Ponca had already been moved to Oklahoma. Standing Bear was jailed briefly for urging the Ponca to resist relocation. In May, about six hundred Ponca, including Standing Bear, were forced to march to Oklahoma at bayonet point. The journey took them fifty days. Nine Ponca died on the way, including Standing Bear's daughter.

In Oklahoma, the Ponca suffered from starvation and malaria, and one-third of them died during the first year, including Standing Bear's son. In the middle of winter, Standing Bear led sixty-six followers away from the reservation. They walked for two months, much of the time barefoot in the snow. Finally they took shelter among the Omaha.

In the spring, General **George Crook** arrested Standing Bear and his followers but was shocked by their condition. When they related their story to him, Crook encouraged **Thomas Henry Tibbles**, a reporter, to publicize the story and file a lawsuit on Standing Bear's behalf.

In the case of *Standing Bear v. Crook*, Judge Elmer Dundy ruled that "An Indian is a person within the meaning of the law, and there is no law giving the army authority to forcibly remove Indians from their lands."

Standing Bear began to travel around the country telling his story with Omaha interpreter **Susette La Flesche** (see no. 45). Eventually he and his followers were allowed to live on their old Nebraska reservation, though most Ponca chose to remain in Oklahoma.

GERONIMO led one of the last bands of Apache to resist relocation to reservations. He fought so bravely and evaded capture for so long, that his name became synonymous with a battle cry charge.

Born **Goyathlay** (One Who Yawns), he lived in an isolated community in the mountains; his childhood was peaceful, undisturbed by any Anglo settlers. As a teenager, he joined **Mangas Coloradas** (see no. 19) and **Cochise** (see no. 26) in battles against **Mexico**. When he turned seventeen, Geronimo joined the council of warriors. In 1858 he went into Mexico to trade. Upon returning home, he discovered that many of his friends and relatives, including his mother, his wife, and his three children, had been killed by Mexican soldiers.

For the next several years, Geronimo raided Mexico regularly, as a means of revenge, as well as to obtain supplies for his community. According to some historians, he got the name Geronimo during these raids when terrified Mexican soldiers called on **St. Jerome** (in Spanish, Jeronimo or Geronimo) to help them. Other historians believe that the name Geronimo was a

Spanish transliteration of Goyathlay. During this time, Geronimo's courage earned him the respect of many warriors in his band.

In the 1870s, the U.S. Army forced thousands of Apache onto the **San Carlos Reservation** in southeast Arizona. For a few years, Geronimo and his followers lived in Mexico. Over the next decade, Geronimo would come and go from the San Carlos Reservation several times. Much of the time, he and his followers lived in Mexico, raiding horses and cattle and killing settlers from the United States and Mexico.

The last time Geronimo left the reservation, in 1885, the army pursued him. In March 1886, he surrendered in Mexico, only to flee with a small group as they approached the border. During this last campaign, Geronimo, sixteen warriors, twelve women, and six children were pursued by five thousand troops. They surrendered five months later, when the U.S. government promised, falsely, that after a short trip to **Florida**, they would be returned to Arizona. Geronimo and his followers were taken to Florida and then **Alabama**, where one-fourth of them died of causes related to unsanitary living conditions.

Though some of his followers were allowed to return to the San Carlos Reservation, Geronimo never saw his home again. The **Comanche** and the **Kiowa**, old enemies of the Apache, offered Geronimo part of their reservation at **Fort Sill**, Oklahoma. Geronimo accepted the offer, became a farmer, and converted to **Christianity**. In 1905 he published his memoirs. He died of pneumonia in 1909.

◆ Warrior, chief, and holy man, the great **Sioux** leader **SITTING BULL** may well be the most famous Native American in history.

As a child, Sitting Bull was nicknamed "Slow," and he worked very hard to disprove the nickname. He became such a renowned warrior that his followers could intimidate their enemies just by shouting, "We are Sitting Bull's boys." In 1867 he became the principal chief of the Sioux, with **Crazy Horse** (see no. 41) as second-in-command.

In 1874 Colonel **George Custer** confirmed the presence of gold in the Black Hills in present-day South Dakota, an area the Sioux considered sacred. The U.S. government offered to buy the land for $6 million, but the Sioux, relying on the research of **Spotted Tail** (see no. 36), asked for $60 million. The government refused and opened the land to miners.

In the middle of winter in 1875–1876, the government sent a message that all Plains Native Americans not on reservations by January 31 would be considered hostile. However, the Sioux could not move 240 miles in bitter cold in just a few weeks. Nevertheless, in March, U.S. troops set out to capture the Sioux.

On June 25, 1876, Custer led his **Seventh Cavalry** in an attack near the **Little Bighorn River** in present-day Montana. He did not realize that Sitting Bull had established an alliance of several thousand Sioux and **Cheyenne**—including more than two thousand warriors. In the most famous battle in history between Native Americans and the U.S. military, Sitting Bull's warriors wiped out Custer's entire 200-man force.

The Sioux continued to win their battles, but they could not win the war. The buffalo, which they needed for food and supplies, was becoming extinct. Most Sioux eventually surrendered, but a few fled with Sitting

Bull into Canada. After four years, even they gave up.

Sitting Bull moved to the **Standing Rock Reservation**, leaving briefly to tour with **Buffalo Bill Cody's** Wild West show. As the U.S. government took more reservation land, Sitting Bull, like **Red Cloud** (see no. 29), campaigned for the government to live up to its treaties.

In the late 1880s, many Sioux began to practice the new Ghost Dance religion, which claimed to be able to restore the Native American way of life. Although the Ghost Dance religion forbade violence, the U.S. government feared its followers would try to foment a rebellion and therefore banned the religion. Sitting Bull supported the **Ghost Dance movement**, and in 1890, Bureau of Indian Affairs agents tried to arrest him. When his warriors tried to prevent the arrest, Sitting Bull was shot and killed. A few weeks later, the remaining dancers were massacred with **Big Foot** (see no. 31) at **Wounded Knee**.

SPOTTED TAIL was a leader of the **Brulé Sioux** during the **Plains Wars** of the late 1800s. He advocated compromising with the U.S. government in order to prevent war but also worked hard to preserve traditional Sioux culture.

Like the Hunkpapa and Oglala Sioux, the Brulé lived in the western Plains states. During Spotted Tail's first years as a warrior, the Sioux were constantly at war with the **Pawnee**, competing with them for access to hunting grounds. Because of his prowess in these battles, Spotted Tail was chosen to be a war leader by the time he was thirty.

In 1855, U.S. troops attacked a Brulé village because a cow belonging to a Mormon emigrant had been killed by a Sioux. Spotted Tail led a retaliatory raid, killing all the men in the unit. More troops came, however, and in larger numbers, killing eighty-six Brulé and capturing seventy, including Spotted Tail's wife and baby daughter. To bring about peace, Spotted Tail and two other leaders went to Fort Laramie to give themselves up, expecting to be executed. Instead, they were imprisoned for about a year in Fort Leavenworth, Kansas. The Sioux respected Spotted Tail for his sacrifice and continued to consider him a war leader.

Spotted Tail allied himself with other Sioux groups who went to war after the massacre of **Black Kettle's** community at Sand Creek in 1864 (see no. 20). However, during Red Cloud's War for the Bozeman Trail, he cooperated with the peace commission, advising the Sioux not to fight. In 1868 Spotted Tail signed the **Treaty of Fort Laramie**, agreeing to a large South Dakota reservation for the Brulé. During the next several years, he frequently traveled with **Red Cloud** to Washington, DC, to lobby on behalf of the Sioux.

When gold was discovered in the Black Hills, the United States offered the Sioux $6 million for the land. Spotted Tail researched its value and asked for $60 million. The government refused. During the war that followed, Spotted Tail tried to negotiate a peace treaty, and eventually did negotiate the peaceful surrender of his nephew, **Crazy Horse** (see no. 41).

On the reservation, Spotted Tail worked to improve the lives of people in his community. He maintained a police force to keep liquor off the reservation and worked hard to prevent the army from relocating the Sioux to Oklahoma. When a Sioux warrior killed a settler, Spotted Tail turned him over to the government, and then used his own money to hire a lawyer for the man's defense. However, in the 1870s, some sub-chiefs plotted to overthrow Spotted Tail, and in 1881 one of them named **Crow Dog**, shot and killed him.

KICKING BIRD was one of several **Kiowa** leaders at a time when the Kiowa were deeply divided over whether to fight for their land or make peace with the settlers. Kicking Bird favored peace and managed to convince most of his people not to go to war.

During Kicking Bird's youth, **Little Mountain** was the principal chief of the Kiowa. Kicking Bird became known as a valiant warrior, but he knew that Little Mountain felt their community's best hope was peace with the United States. In 1865 he signed the Treaty of the Little Arkansas River, accepting a reservation in the Oklahoma panhandle.

Little Mountain died in 1866, leaving Kicking Bird as the leader of the peace faction of Kiowa, and **Satanta** as the leader of the war faction. As a compromise, the community chose **Lone Wolf**, a militant leader who sometimes advocated peace, as their principal chief; but the two factions continued to struggle for control of the tribe.

In 1867 Lone Wolf and Kicking Bird both attended a peace conference with representatives of the U.S. government, as well as the Cheyenne, Arapaho, Comanche, Kiowa, and Kiowa Apache nations. Both leaders signed a treaty agreeing to a new, smaller reservation and the establishment of individual farm plots for families.

The following year, a group of Cheyenne were massacred at **Sand Creek**, making Kicking Bird even more determined to pursue a policy of peace. Members of the war faction began to call him a coward, so Kicking Bird led a raid into Texas, robbing a stagecoach and attacking an army unit.

The Texas raid was to be Kicking Bird's last act of violence. In the following years, he worked to promote peace. In 1873 he negotiated the release of Satanta and **Big Tree**, who had been arrested. This act earned him the loyalty of many people in his community.

He prevented most Kiowa from joining their allies, the Comanche, in their war of 1873–1874.

Lone Wolf did go to war, however, and members of the war faction of the Kiowa constantly pressured Kicking Bird to consider war. In 1874, though, the warring Kiowa were defeated, and Kicking Bird helped negotiate their surrender. The U.S. Army asked Kicking Bird to identify the ringleaders to be imprisoned, and he named Lone Wolf and **Mamanti**.

Before he was taken to prison, Mamanti denounced Kicking Bird and threatened him. A few days later, Kicking Bird became ill while drinking a cup of coffee. Within a few hours, he was dead. An army doctor thought he had died of strychnine poisoning, and many Kiowa believed that his death was caused by Mamanti.

DAT SO LA LEE was one of the greatest weavers of the **Washoe**, a nation renowned for their fine baskets. Today, her baskets are worth hundreds of thousands of dollars.

The Washoe traditionally create fine baskets out of fern fibers and willow reed. The baskets, which incorporate complex geometrical designs, are very difficult to make. The weaver uses her teeth, fingers, a piece of sharp stone, and an awl to sew thirty-six stitches per inch. Dat So La Lee learned this skill at a young age and became very good at it. People said that she had "magic fingers."

However, when she was still a teenager, the Washoe lost a war with the **Paiute**, and the Paiute banned the Washoe from basket weaving. The Paiute wanted to sell their own baskets without competition from the Washoe weavers. Because the Washoe economy was based on selling and trading baskets, the next fifty years were a time of extreme poverty for them.

Despite the ban, Dat So La Lee and other Washoe women did not stop weaving baskets. However, since she was unable to sell her work, Dat So La Lee grew poor along with the rest of the Washoe. She married twice—her first husband died only a few years after they were married—and had several children.

In 1895 when her family had become critically poor, Dat So La Lee decided to defy the Paiute ban. She took some glass bottles she had covered with weaving to Carson City and sold them to **Abram and Amy Cohn**, who owned a store there. From then on, the Cohns took charge of marketing Dat So La Lee's work for her. Dat So La Lee's baskets were remarkably well made and came to be prized by collectors everywhere. Her original, geometrical designs were tiny and required exact spacing. She made innovative changes to traditional designs, working with a new type of basket that was an incurving spheroid, and adding two-color design to her repertoire.

Dat So La Lee, who was very religious, apparently saw her designs first in visions and dreams. One of her most famous baskets, called "Myriads of Stars Shine Over the Graves of Our Ancestors," took her more than a year to complete. It contains 56,590 stitches and sold for $10,000 in 1930.

In her old age, Dat So La Lee lost much of her vision, but she continued to weave until she died at the age of ninety. During her life, she produced nearly three hundred baskets, including forty extremely large pieces that came to be known as the "great treasures." Many of these large pieces are exhibited in museums around the world and, when sold in recent years, have cost as much as $250,000.

LOZEN, the sister of **Victorio** (see no. 30), was unusual among **Apache** women because she chose never to marry, and instead devoted herself to living as a warrior.

Many Apache women went to war, but they normally assisted male warriors by setting up camp, cooking, and caring for those who were injured. Lozen did those things too, but she was also a renowned fighter. Victorio described her as his "right hand," "strong as a man" and "braver than most." Respected as a **Holy Woman**, Lozen sat on decision-making councils, and when the legendary Apache chief **Geronimo** (see no. 34) decided to surrender, he sent Lozen and her companion **Dahteste**, another woman warrior, to arrange it.

During Lozen's childhood, even though Apache adult gender roles varied, young girls and boys both were taught to run, hunt, fight, follow tracks, and ride a horse. Both also learned to cook and sew. This occurred because it was expected that at times, their survival might depend on that knowledge. So as a child, Lozen learned horsemanship and how to use weapons. She often won foot races against boys her age.

Like other Apache girls, during her puberty ceremony, Lozen climbed into the mountains and fasted there for four days and four nights. While there, she was said to have been visited by spirits who gave her two powers: the ability to find the location of an enemy, and the ability to heal wounds. She was renowned for these abilities the rest of her life.

Legend has it that Victorio's band relied on Lozen's powers to evade the U.S. and Mexican armies. She would look toward the sky, stretch out her arms, and turn in a circle while singing a prayer. Her hands would begin to tingle when she turned in the direction of a foreign army. When Victorio's

band was defeated, Lozen was away helping a pregnant woman return to her family. Several warriors from the group believed they could not have been cornered if Lozen had been with them.

After Victorio's death, Lozen joined Geronimo's band, among whom she soon developed a reputation for bravery. During one battle, she risked her life to recover a dropped bag of bullets because the band was low on ammunition. Like the other warriors, however, Lozen knew that she could not survive as a fugitive forever.

At Geronimo's request, Lozen helped set up peace negotiations. After the 1886 surrender, she was manacled and sent to **Fort Marion**, Florida, with Geronimo. The following year the band was moved to Mobile, Alabama, where unsanitary living conditions resulted in the death of one out of every four of them, including Lozen, who died of tuberculosis.

CHIEF JOSEPH, the younger Joseph of the **Nez Percé**, helped lead his people on what is considered the most brilliant retreat in the history of Native American–U.S. military warfare.

The Nez Percé, who lived in **Idaho**, eastern **Oregon**, and **Washington**, had been at peace with the United States ever since Lewis and Clark first visited their lands in the early 1800s. They kept the peace even when settlers stole their horses and cattle. Joseph's father, **Joseph the Elder**, converted to **Christianity**, and young Joseph attended a mission school as a child.

According to an 1855 treaty, the Nez Percé were entitled to remain on a large reservation in their home territory. However, in 1863 gold was discovered in northeast Oregon—where Joseph lived. The U.S. government then convinced a few Nez Percé to sign a treaty reducing their territory by almost six million acres; they also agreed to move to an Idaho reservation. Joseph the Elder did not sign the treaty and, in a rage, tore his copy to pieces.

Joseph the Elder did not move his people to Idaho and neither did his son, who became a leader of the Nez Percé after his father died. In 1877 General **Oliver Howard** threatened the Nez Percé and gave them a month to leave. To keep the peace, they prepared to go. However, then a few angry young warriors killed some white settlers. Expecting the entire community to be punished for the actions of a few, the Nez Percé decided to flee to **Canada**.

Some two hundred Nez Percé warriors and around five hundred women, old people, and children journeyed more than 1,500 miles through Washington, Oregon, Idaho, and Montana, crossing the Rocky Mountains twice. Pursued by ten separate army commands, they defeated or fought to a standoff the two thousand soldiers who followed them in thirteen battles and skirmishes, using such skill that cadets at West Point still study their tactics.

The Nez Percé leaders included several chiefs besides Joseph, and they would plan their strategy in war council meetings. However, as the retreat progressed, it was Joseph who became a symbol of the Nez Percé resistance. As they continued to elude capture and defeat, newspapers compared him to Napoleon.

The Nez Percé War lasted through the summer and fall of 1877. The long trek ended when General **Nelson Miles** surprised the Nez Percé thirty miles from the Canadian border. At first, they were taken to Oklahoma, where many died of malaria. Joseph was eventually allowed to move to the **Colville Reservation** in Washington State. He made two trips to Washington, DC, to speak on behalf of the Nez Percé before he died in 1904.

As chief of the **Lakota Sioux**, **CRAZY HORSE** led his people to the most famous Native American victory over the U.S. Army in American history.

As a child, Crazy Horse was called **Curly**, because he had curly hair. At the time, the name Crazy Horse referred to his father. When Curly was around thirteen, he was living with his uncle, **Spotted Tail** (see no. 36). One day Curly watched as a group of soldiers attacked Sioux leaders who were trying peacefully to mediate a dispute. Spotted Tail then led a group of warriors who killed the soldiers.

Sometime later, Curly was away from the village, hunting buffalo. When he returned, the village was a burned wreck, and eighty-six people lay dead. He rescued the one person he found alive, a Cheyenne woman. About four miles away, Curly found more survivors, who told him U.S. cavalry had attacked the village.

Curly returned to Lakota territory in 1857. That year he performed many daring feats

in a battle with the **Crow.** To recognize his son's deeds, Curly's father gave him his own name, Crazy Horse. His skills as a warrior were about to be tested.

In 1864 the Lakota learned of the Sand Creek massacre of Black Kettle's Cheyenne (see no. 20). At the same time, the U.S. Army was beginning to build a road through Lakota territory to reach Montana's goldfields. With **Red Cloud** (see no. 29) as their leader, the Lakota went to war and forced the army to abandon the project. After the war, Red Cloud agreed to live on a reservation, and Crazy Horse became the war chief of the **Oglala,** a band of the Lakota.

In 1876 Crazy Horse received the U.S. government's message ordering the rest of the Sioux to move onto reservations. Instead, he joined **Sitting Bull** and the ten thousand Sioux and Cheyenne who were camped with him on the **Little Bighorn River**. When Colonel **George Custer** attacked on June 25, Crazy Horse led the band who killed Custer and his more than two hundred soldiers.

In retaliation, U.S. military reinforcements were quickly sent to pursue the Sioux, who continued to win other battles. However, Sitting Bull and Crazy Horse were running out of supplies, and the buffalo were dying. Sitting Bull left for Canada, but Crazy Horse led his followers to Red Cloud's reservation.

A few months later, after departing the reservation, Crazy Horse was arrested and murdered by a white soldier who stabbed him with a bayonet after he tried to escape.

Activist **SARAH WINNEMUCCA** is often considered the most famous Native American woman of the nineteenth century. For most of her life, she worked to obtain fair treatment for the **Paiute.**

When Winnemucca was born, the Paiute lived in the desert region shared by Nevada, Oregon, and California. They had never met American settlers, because settlers usually journeyed around the desert. However, Winnemucca's grandfather, **Chief Winnemucca,** guided American explorer **John Frémont** to California, and as a child, Winnemucca sometimes traveled there with her grandfather. She learned to speak English, Spanish, and several Native American languages.

Because of her language proficiency, Winnemucca often interpreted for her father when he met with U.S. Indian agents in charge of the reservations, army officers, and Native American leaders from other nations. She was confined to a reservation during the Paiute War of 1860 but worked for the army during later conflicts. She advocated peace between the Paiute and the U.S. government, but violence continued to break out periodically; some historians believe Winnemucca's mother, sister, and brother were killed by soldiers.

Winnemucca frequently spoke out about abuses by Indian agents. Like many Indian agents, the agents in charge of the Paiute reservation were corrupt. They stole food and supplies from the Paiute, and did not stop white settlers from squatting on their lands. The Paiute grew poor, and in 1875, they were moved to Oregon's **Malheur Reservation.**

In 1878 some Paiute decided to join a related nation, Idaho's Bannock, in a war against the U.S. government. Winnemucca, however, became an army interpreter and scout. After the war, the government decided that all the Paiute involved in the war, regardless of which side they were on, should be relocated to Washington's **Yakama Reservation**.

They were forced to travel the 350 miles to Yakama in the middle of winter. Lacking winter clothing, many Paiute died along the way, and others died shortly after their arrival because the housing and food on the reservation were so inadequate.

To call attention to the Paiute plight, Winnemucca delivered a series of lectures in San Francisco. She also wrote a book, *Life Among the Piutes* [sic], which was the first published work written in English by a Native American woman.

President **Rutherford B. Hayes** agreed to meet with her, and his secretary of the interior promised Winnemucca that the Paiute could return to Malheur; however, funding for the move was not provided, and the Yakama agent refused to let the Paiutes leave. The next year, the U.S. government opened Malheur to settlers.

In her last years, Winnemucca taught school and lectured along the East Coast. She died of tuberculosis in 1891.

QUANAH PARKER led the **Quahadi** band of the **Comanche** in a war to save the buffalo. After the war, he became an important peacetime leader for the Comanche.

In 1836 the Comanche raided Fort Parker, a Texas settlement, and captured nine-year-old **Cynthia Ann Parker**. They raised her, and she grew to consider herself a Comanche. Eventually she married a Comanche chief, **Peta Nocona**. With him, she had two sons, **Pecos** and Quanah, and a daughter, **Topsannah**.

In 1860 their lives were torn apart. Texas Rangers captured Cynthia Ann and Topsannah and fatally wounded Peta Nocona. The Rangers returned Cynthia Ann to the Parker family. In the next few years, she tried to escape several times and then, after Topsannah died, is said to have died of a broken heart. Among the Comanche, Quanah's brother Pecos grew ill and died.

The next several years were difficult for Quanah as he mourned the loss of his family. However, he polished his hunting and war skills and became a chief. It was also a difficult time for the Comanche nation. In 1867 the government called for the Comanche, **Cheyenne**, **Kiowa**, **Kiowa Apache**, and **Arapaho** to settle on reservations in **Oklahoma**. Most Comanche did, but the Quahadi branch refused; they continued to live off the buffalo, and periodically raided frontier towns for seven years. During that time, the Quahadi grew ever more desperate as professional buffalo hunters gradually destroyed the herds.

In 1874 Quanah and other Comanche, Kiowa, Cheyenne, and Arapaho leaders led seven hundred warriors in an attack against twenty-eight buffalo hunters at **Adobe Walls**, beginning what came to be known as the **Red River War**. The buffalo hunters were armed with a cannon and with the newest technology—repeating rifles with a 600-yard range—and the warriors were forced to retreat. A few months later, the army captured or killed 1,500 of the militants' horses and destroyed their tepees. In June 1875, Quanah and his band turned themselves in and relocated to Indian Territory in Oklahoma.

Quanah quickly adjusted to reservation life. He took up farming and ranching, began using his mother's last name, and learned to speak Spanish and English. He also became a peacetime leader of his community, negotiating leasing rights when cattle ranchers and investors wanted to use Comanche pastures.

Quanah persuaded the federal government to recognize him as the principal chief of the Comanche. As such, he frequently traveled to Washington, DC, to represent Comanche interests, and he arranged to share the Comanche reservation with **Geronimo**. When Parker died in 1911, he was so beloved that the line of mourners following his funeral procession was more than a mile long.

The last chief of the **Crow**, **PLENTY COUPS** was their leader during their transition to reservation life.

When he was fourteen, Plenty Coups went into the mountains to do a vision quest. In his vision, he saw the buffalo disappear, while cattle appeared in their place. Then there was a storm that only a chickadee survived. Plenty Coups and his community believed the dream meant that settlers would take over the Plains, and that like the chickadee, the Crow could survive.

Because of his vision, Plenty Coups urged his community never to go to war against the United States. However, he did wage war against other Native American nations, especially the **Lakota**, who had killed two of his brothers and his parents. He was granted the name Plenty Coups after performing eighty heroic acts in battle.

Plenty Coups became a chief around the age of twenty-five. During the **Plains Wars**—the wars during the 1860s and 1870s between the United States and Plains nations such as the Sioux and the Cheyenne—he and other Crow warriors served as scouts for the U.S. Army. Crow warriors also assisted the army in its campaign against Joseph and the Nez Percé (see no. 40).

The early decision of the Crow to cooperate with the U.S. government may have helped them avoid the tragic fate that befell some of their traditional enemies. The Crow were granted a reservation in their homeland in southern **Montana**. On the reservation, Plenty Coups for the first time stepped into the role of peacetime leader. He encouraged the Crow to take up farming and ranching but to also continue practicing the traditional Crow religion. Plenty Coups also continued to advocate Crow interests within the United States. For example, when railroad companies wanted to lay tracks across Crow territory, he insisted that the railroads hire Crow to work for them.

In his final years, Plenty Coups often negotiated with government representatives. He pressed for the Crow to receive a share of the profits when their land was leased to oil and gas companies. When Congress tried to open the Crow reservation to settlers, Plenty Coups traveled to Washington, DC, at least ten times to fight the plan, and he succeeded in blocking it.

In his will, Plenty Coups dedicated his farmland and home to be a memorial and museum for the Crow nation, to be "a reminder to Indians and white people alike that the two races should live and work together harmoniously." When he died in 1932, the Crow showed their respect for Plenty Coups by eliminating the title "chief," to make sure that he would be the last Crow leader ever to hold that honor.

Teacher, author, and lecturer, **SUSETTE LA FLESCHE** was an activist who worked tirelessly to advance the rights of Native Americans.

La Flesche grew up on the **Omaha** Reservation in Nebraska. She attended the Presbyterian mission school on the reservation. Next, she traveled to New Jersey to attend the **Elizabeth Institute for Young Ladies**, becoming the first Omaha to seek her education outside her homeland.

After she graduated, La Flesche applied for a job teaching at a reservation school. At first, she did not get the job, but then she learned that reservation schools were required by law to hire qualified Native Americans if they applied. La Flesche wrote an angry letter to the Commissioner of Indian Affairs and was quickly hired.

In 1877 **Standing Bear** (see no. 33) led a group of **Ponca** from Indian Territory in Oklahoma back to Nebraska. The Ponca and Omaha nations are closely related, so the Ponca took refuge among the Omaha. However, the army caught up with the Ponca and put them in jail, in preparation for sending them back to their reservation. The *Omaha Daily Herald* publicized their plight, and several lawyers volunteered to help them sue the army.

At the trial, La Flesche testified on behalf of the Ponca, and she wrote several articles about the case. The court ruled that the Ponca could not be jailed without just cause, a decision that recognized for the first time that Native Americans have rights in United States law. Following the trial, La Flesche, her brother **Francis**, and reporter **Thomas Henry Tibbles** toured the country with Standing Bear.

On the lecture tour, Susette and Francis interpreted for Standing Bear; Susette also gave lectures, and soon became a national celebrity known as "**Bright Eyes**." She advocated making Native Americans citizens, and called for the allotment of reservation lands to individual owners. La Flesche feared that the government could take land away from a nation much more easily than it could from individual citizens.

Thanks in part to her efforts, the U.S. government began a policy of land allotment. However, it did not seem to help, as swindlers often tricked new landowners into turning over the title to their lands. During this time, La Flesche also wrote a book with Standing Bear, *Ploughed Under: The Story of an Indian Chief*.

After the lecture tour ended, La Flesche and Tibbles married. They continued to give lectures, raising awareness about living conditions on reservations. In 1886 they lectured in England and Scotland. A few years later, they reported together on the **Wounded Knee massacre.** They frequently lobbied Congress on behalf of the Omaha and Ponca. La Flesche died in 1903.

Although his childhood education consisted of only a few years of mission school, **FRANCIS LA FLESCHE** became one of the first Native Americans to become a successful scholar and ethnologist.

Like his famous sisters **Susan** (see no. 51) and **Susette** (see no. 45), Francis La Flesche grew up on the **Omaha Reservation** in Nebraska. His father, **Joseph La Flesche**, the principal chief of the Omaha nation, made sure that Francis participated in traditional activities such as buffalo hunts and religious ceremonies. However, Joseph La Flesche had also converted to **Presbyterianism**, and he required his children to attend the reservation's Presbyterian mission school and learn English. He raised his children in a manner that allowed them to function within both the Native American and white cultures.

Because they were fluent in English, La Flesche and his sister Susette were able to interpret for **Ponca** chief **Standing Bear** when he toured the country giving lectures. On the tour, La Flesche met **Alice Cunningham Fletcher**, a famous ethnologist and Native American rights activist. He and Fletcher became close friends. After the tour, La Flesche went to work in Washington, DC, as a clerk in the **Bureau of Indian Affairs**.

While he was working there, La Flesche spent his spare time researching Omaha culture with Fletcher. He traveled with her to Nebraska and interpreted for her among the Omaha. He persuaded several Omaha elders to explain the words and rituals for several religious ceremonies to both of them.

During the years of his association with Fletcher, La Flesche worked hard. In addition to his research on the Omaha, he returned to school, earning a bachelor's degree in law from National University in 1892 and a master's degree the following year. In 1893 he and Fletcher coauthored *A Study of Omaha Music*, and in 1900 he published his own book, *The Middle Five*, a description of what it was like to attend a mission school on the Omaha Reservation.

In 1910 he transferred from the Bureau of Indian Affairs to the Smithsonian's **Bureau of American Ethnology**. There he could devote himself to ethnological research full time. In 1911 he and Fletcher published an exhaustive study of the Omaha, based on their research over the previous twenty years, called *The Omaha Tribe*.

La Flesche then began to study the **Osage**, a nation closely related to the Omaha. In his later years, after Fletcher's death in 1923, La Flesche published several important works on the Osage, including a *Dictionary of the Osage Language*.

La Flesche received many professional honors for his scholarship. He was a member of the National Academy of Sciences and was granted an honorary doctorate from the University of Nebraska. He died on the Omaha Reservation in 1932.

HENRY CHEE DODGE was the last official Head Chief of the **Navajo** and their first **Tribal Chairman**. He was also a successful businessman and rancher.

Dodge's father died when he was very young. When he was about six, legendary frontiersman **Kit Carson**, who was a colonel in the New Mexico Volunteers Regiment, began destroying crops and livestock in order to force the Navajo to move to the **Bosque Redondo** Reservation in **New Mexico**. Dodge's family fled.

One day, Dodge's mother left the camp to look for food and to ask her **Hopi** relatives to shelter the family. She never returned. Dodge was passed from family to family and finally, because of a mix-up, was accidentally left alone beside the trail. He met an eight-year-old girl and her grandfather, who adopted him; they took him with them to Bosque Redondo, where they lived for four years until the Navajo were allowed to return home.

Dodge and his new family returned to the area around **Fort Defiance** in New Mexico, where he was reunited with one of his aunts. There, he learned English and Spanish and attended the Fort Defiance Indian School. Then he began working as a translator at his uncle's trading post. Eventually he became the official Navajo interpreter for the U.S. Army.

In 1883 Dodge became the chief of the Navajo police, often interpreting during police investigations and mediating to prevent violent incidents. The following year, the government appointed Dodge as head chief of the Navajo, though he was not yet recognized as a leader by the Navajo communities.

Head chief was not a high-paying position, but since Dodge was unmarried, he managed to save most of his earnings from his various jobs. By 1890 he could afford to invest in a trading post and sheep ranch. After his business was established, he married and eventually had five children.

In the 1920s, Dodge and two other Navajo businessmen formed a council to handle requests for oil exploration leases on reservation land. From this council, the new **Navajo Tribal Council** was born, and in 1923 Dodge was elected as its first chairman. The council protected Navajo interests in negotiations with the U.S. government and with private corporations. In 1927 Dodge convinced Congress that the Navajo should receive 100 percent of the royalties from oil found under the reservation.

In 1928 Dodge resigned as council chairman to attend to his ranch. He was reelected to the council in 1942 and again in 1946 but never took office after his last election. He contracted pneumonia and died the following year.

CHARLES ALEXANDER EASTMAN was one of the first Native Americans to earn an MD, but he was to become known as much for his writing as for his medical practice.

Eastman was left without his parents at an early age. His mother died giving birth to him, and when he was four, his father was sentenced to death for his role in the wars between the **Sioux** and the United States.

Eastman fled with his grandmother and uncle into **Canada**. In his book *Indian Boyhood*, Eastman later described the thorough education he received among the Sioux in Manitoba, and the care his uncle took to help him become an astute observer of nature.

Throughout his childhood, Eastman expected that someday he would have to avenge his father's death. What he didn't realize was that his father had never been executed; President **Abraham Lincoln** had pardoned him, and he was then serving time in an Iowa penitentiary.

When Eastman's father was released from prison, he immediately searched for his fifteen-year-old son and brought him to live in the United States.

Eastman's father insisted that he enroll in a mission school. The contrast between Eastman's school days and his former life was extreme, but he was a good student and went on to attend Beloit College, Knox College, and Dartmouth College, where he earned a bachelor's degree in 1887. He then went straight to medical school at Boston University, earning his degree in 1890.

Right after graduation, Eastman became the doctor for the **Pine Ridge Reservation** in South Dakota. He was the only doctor to treat the victims of the massacre of Big Foot's band at **Wounded Knee**, an experience that shocked him.

After three years working at Pine Ridge, Eastman opened a private medical practice. It was difficult to earn a living as a Native American doctor, however, because many settlers had racist attitudes toward Native Americans, and very few Sioux could afford to pay a doctor. In 1895 he went to work for the **YMCA**, organizing thirty-two programs for Native American young people. Perhaps influenced by his wife, poet **Elaine Goodale**, he also began to write.

Over the next twenty-seven years Eastman wrote ten books and numerous articles on Native American culture and life. He also continued to practice medicine and to work on behalf of the Sioux, lobbying on their behalf in Washington, DC. He worked on a Bureau of Indian Affairs project to give the Sioux legal names to protect their interests and served as a U.S. Indian inspector for reservations. He spent the last decade of his life lecturing in the United States and in England.

NAMPEYO, a **Tewa** potter, was perhaps the first Native American artist to become nationally and internationally famous for her work.

At a time when most women in her community had stopped adding decorative artwork to their pots, Nampeyo restored pottery making to its status as an art form. Because of her influence, Hopi women began to earn an income by making and selling pottery, improving the **Hopi** economy. Nampeyo lived at Hano, a Tewa-Hopi community at First Mesa, one of the Three Mesas in northeastern Arizona where the Tewa and Hopi have lived for hundreds of years. There was no school in her area when Nampeyo was growing up. Like most children in her community at that time, she spent her days helping to carry water, grind corn, and plant crops.

Nampeyo learned to make pots by watching her grandmother make pots for carrying water. Nampeyo was fascinated by the process of collecting the clay, grinding it, and then shaping a pot by spiraling ropes of clay upward from the base. She was lucky to have the chance to learn this art, because by this time many Hopi women had begun to use metal pots and china bowls. Fewer and fewer of them were making their own pots.

Because the Hopi lived in the same area their ancestors had, Nampeyo could find very old fragments of pottery to study. In 1895 her husband helped archaeologists excavate an ancient **Pueblo** site. She studied the shards of pottery he found, sketching the designs she saw there. Later, she visited other archaeological sites in order to study more ancient pots.

Nampeyo began to decorate her own pots with designs inspired by the ancient potters. She used traditional methods to make the pots, prospecting for clay, pounding it with stones, removing impurities, and adding sand. She painted her pots, using yucca brushes that she made herself, and fired them in a traditional outdoor oven so hot that she had to wet her hair first in order to withstand the temperatures.

Other women criticized Nampeyo's innovative pots. However, wealthy tourists bought so many of them that other potters began to copy her work. Nampeyo became famous, making trips to the **Grand Canyon** and to **Chicago** to demonstrate her pottery-making methods. In recent years, her work has been exhibited at the **Smithsonian Institution** and in museums around the world.

Late in her life, Nampeyo grew blind, probably because of an eye infection resulting from poor sanitary conditions. She kept making pots by touch, and her husband and daughters painted the pots for her. After she died in 1942, seventy-three family members continued to make pots decorated in her style.

CHARLES CURTIS was the first Native American elected to the **U.S. Senate** and the first to become **vice president** of the United States.

Curtis was only one-eighth **Kaw**, but his mother made sure he was listed on the tribal rolls and planned for him to live on the reservation. She did not want Curtis to be excluded from any Kaw land settlements. When Curtis was three years old, however, his mother died. From then on, his Curtis grandparents and his Kaw grandparents, Louis and Julie Pappan, shared custody of him.

Curtis spoke Kaw and fit comfortably into reservation life. He also enjoyed living in Topeka, where Grandfather Curtis owned a racetrack. At the age of nine, Curtis rode in his first race, and he soon became a famous jockey.

In 1873 Curtis left Topeka to meet the Pappans, who were traveling with the rest of the Kaw to Indian Territory in Oklahoma. Curtis wanted to live with the Pappans, but both his grandmothers wanted him to finish school in Kansas, which he did. Afterward, he went to law school.

In 1884 Curtis entered politics; he ran for office and became the county attorney for Shawnee County. In 1892 he was elected to the **U.S. House of Representatives**. He served on the Territories Committee and the Committee on Indian Affairs.

During Curtis's lifetime, some Native Americans fought to maintain the sovereignty of their nations, while others, including Curtis, felt individual Native Americans would be better off assimilated into mainstream American culture. Curtis advocated a policy of allotment, which meant dissolving tribal governments and parceling out tribal land to individual members of each Native American nation.

In 1898 he drafted the **Curtis Act** which abolished tribal courts, prevented tribal laws from being enforced in federal courts, and specifically allotted the lands and dissolved the governments of the **Cherokee**, **Choctaw**, **Chickasaw**, **Creek**, and **Seminole** nations. (In recent times, both tribal courts and tribal governments have been restored.)

In 1907 Curtis was elected to the U.S. Senate. He served there for twenty years, and in 1923 was elected **Senate majority leader**.

In the 1928 presidential race, Curtis was a candidate for the Republican nomination against **Herbert Hoover**. Curtis ran a quiet campaign, hoping to emerge as a compromise candidate. However, when Hoover won the nomination, party loyalists wanted someone from a farm state to balance the ticket, and Curtis and Hoover were stuck with each other. They won the election, but Curtis never played an important role as Hoover's vice president.

After he and Hoover lost the 1932 election to the Democratic ticket headed by Franklin D. Roosevelt, Curtis retired from politics.

◆ **SUSAN LA FLESCHE** was the first Native American woman to become a doctor trained in Western medicine. As the reservation physician for the **Omaha**, she also frequently represented them in negotiations with the U.S. government.

La Flesche was raised on the Omaha Reservation and attended a mission school there. As a teenager, she followed in the footsteps of her sister **Susette** (see no. 45), traveling to New Jersey to attend the **Elizabeth Institute for Young Ladies**. In 1884 Susan enrolled at the **Hampton Institute**, a school that was originally founded to educate freed African American slaves.

After graduation, she obtained a scholarship to the **Woman's Medical College** of Pennsylvania. Her decision to become a doctor was notable not only because there were very few Native American or women physicians at the time but also because the Omaha tradition was for men, not women, to become healers.

La Flesche graduated at the top of her class and soon became the reservation physician for the Omaha. At the time, it was rare for Native Americans to be appointed to such a post, and La Flesche was the first Native American woman to hold such a position.

As the only doctor for 1,300 people, La Flesche worked from dawn until well after dark each day, driving her horse and buggy over miles of country roads to reach her patients. She managed to contain several epidemics of smallpox, influenza, and diphtheria, but she also worked so hard that she damaged her own health. In 1893 La Flesche resigned her post in order to recover and to care for her sick mother.

In 1894 La Flesche married **Henry Picotte**, despite her parents' objection that Picotte was known to be a heavy drinker.

She opened a private practice in **Bancroft, Nebraska,** and continued to work hard, caring for her patients, raising two sons, and giving lectures about health-related issues.

Her husband died in 1905 of an alcohol-related illness, and La Flesche became a **Presbyterian missionary** to the Omaha. She also became an informal representative for the Omaha in negotiations with the government. In one case she traveled to Washington, DC, even though she was terribly ill, after Omaha officials begged her to do so. In Washington she met with the secretary of the interior and convinced him that Omaha landowners should be able to control their own property, rather than have it held in trust on their behalf.

La Flesche's final accomplishment was the opening of a hospital in Walthill, Nebraska. She had campaigned for years to get the hospital built; she died there in 1915 after a long illness.

AMOS BAD HEART BULL is known as the "**Herodotus** of his people," the **Oglala Lakota**, one of the **Sioux** nations. Like that historian of ancient Greece, Bad Heart Bull documented decades of Oglala history, and his chronicles included illustrations and captions.

Bad Heart Bull's father was the Oglala's official historian, recording important events from each year on buffalo hide. However, he died young, and Bad Heart Bull was raised by his uncles. They told him stories about important battles they had fought. As a child, Bad Heart Bull loved to listen to these stories and collected copies of treaties and other documents relating to negotiations between the Lakota and the United States. He never went to school but taught himself how to draw. He also taught himself to read and write, using symbols that missionaries used to transcribe Lakota words. In 1890 Bad Heart Bull enlisted in the U.S. Army as a scout and learned English.

At some point, Bad Heart Bull obtained a used ledger. At the time, paper was a precious commodity, and Native American artists frequently painted and drew in used ledger books. This was such a common practice that for a time, all Native American art on paper was called "ledger art."

Bad Heart Bull used his ledger book to begin a series of 415 drawings. For the next twenty years, he worked at recording the history of the Oglala. He gathered information from people who had lived through historical events, listening to their stories. Then he created illustrations depicting the events, and wrote captions explaining what was happening in each picture. He also drew the only known picture of his cousin, **Crazy Horse** (see no. 41).

Bad Heart Bull's technical skill as an artist was extraordinary. He first drew a

panoramic long-shot view of an event. Then he added framed close-ups, set off to one side so the viewer could see the effects of the event on individual people who were there. His pictures form an invaluable record for historians today for two reasons. He captured small details of everyday Oglala life, and he presented events very objectively, bringing the accounts of many people into a unified whole.

Little is known about Bad Heart Bull's life apart from his work. He died in 1913, and his ledger book passed to his sister, **Dolly Pretty Cloud**. In 1926 University of Nebraska graduate student **Helen Blish** persuaded Pretty Cloud to let her study and photograph it. The photographs were published as the book *A Pictographic History of the Oglala Sioux*. The original was buried with Pretty Cloud when she died in 1947.

Writer and activist **GERTRUDE SIMMONS BONNIN** helped bring about important reforms in U.S. policy toward Native Americans.

Gertrude Simmons was born on the **Yankton Sioux Reservation** in South Dakota, in the same year as the Battle of the Little Bighorn. She grew up at a time when U.S. Indian agents and missionaries were pushing Native Americans to give up their culture. Simmons and her mother resisted this process.

Against her mother's wishes, however, Simmons enrolled in a boarding school run by **Quaker** missionaries. She did not speak English, and teachers beat students if they spoke Sioux, so Simmons had a difficult time there. She learned English, however, and remained at the school for several years.

Simmons then enrolled at Earlham College and began studying to be a teacher. She taught briefly at Carlisle, a school for Native Americans in Pennsylvania. She left the school, though, because its founder believed that Native Americans should be trained as farmers or laborers, not educated in academic subjects.

Simmons moved to Boston, and while

there she began submitting short stories and essays to magazines, using the pseudonym *Zitkala-Sa*, or *Red Bird*. She was published in several national periodicals, including *Harper's* magazine and the *Atlantic Monthly*. In her writings, she criticized the educational practices of white reformers.

In 1902 Simmons married **Richard Bonnin**, who like Simmons was a Nakota, or Yankton, Sioux. They moved to Utah, where they both worked for the **Bureau of Indian Affairs**. Disturbed by the poverty she saw on reservations, Bonnin began working with the **Society of American Indians**. She became SAI's secretary and moved to Washington, DC, so she could lobby Congress on its behalf.

Bonnin resigned from SAI in 1920, but she continued to work as an activist. During the 1920s, she persuaded a women's club to form the **Indian Welfare Committee**. This committee studied reservation living conditions—which in many cases were severely poor—and pressured the U.S. government to conduct a follow-up investigation. As a result, Congress hired a research firm that verified many of the Indian Welfare Committee's findings. The firm's report, called the **Meriam Report**, led to important reforms in government policy.

At the same time, Bonnin was working with the **Indian Rights Association** to study the theft of land from Native Americans in Oklahoma. In 1924 she cowrote an exposé showing that swindlers had tricked many Native Americans into giving up land on which oil had been discovered.

During Bonnin's lifetime, Congress did pass some of the legal reforms she had worked so hard to bring about. In 1924 Native Americans were granted U.S. citizenship. In 1934 Congress allocated money to pay for healthcare and schools on reservations.

◆ **Cherokee** humorist **WILL ROGERS** was one of the most beloved entertainers of the early twentieth century.

Rogers grew up on his family's ranch in present-day **Oklahoma**. He went to his first cattle roundup as a toddler and learned to throw a rope before he was five years old. Rogers loved to do rope tricks and won his first prize for roping at the age of twenty. So it's no surprise that he began his career as an entertainer doing rope tricks in Wild West shows.

As a young man, he worked as a cowhand and managed his father's ranch, but in 1901 he left for Argentina. He traveled the world, tending cattle and working in Wild West shows and circuses in South Africa, New Zealand, and Australia. Then he returned to America and became a "rope artist and rough rider" in various Wild West shows.

One day, Rogers began telling jokes about current events as he did his tricks. Rogers loved reading newspapers and found enough material there to provide jokes for three daily performances. He didn't confine himself to joking about current events, however. For example, Rogers was proud of his Cherokee ancestry and sometimes remarked, "My ancestors didn't come over on the *Mayflower*, but they met the boat."

Audiences loved Rogers's down-to-earth, nonpartisan approach to entertainment. By 1912 he had begun appearing onstage and then later in movies, and was a big success in both. In 1922 he started writing a humorous column on the news for the *New York Times*. For a while he was the most widely read newspaper columnist of his day. In 1930 he began a weekly radio show.

Many people admired Rogers for his efforts to help charitable causes. He gave the **Red Cross** $100 per week for the duration of World War I. During the Depression, he donated a percentage of his earnings from each radio broadcast to the Red Cross and the **Salvation Army**. At various times, he gave performances to benefit flood victims, earthquake victims, farmers, and the unemployed.

Rogers was one of the country's earliest flying enthusiasts. He flew to most of his engagements around the country, at a time when few U.S. planes carried passengers and most people considered flying to be dangerous. If he could not catch a passenger flight, he would ride a mail plane, weighing himself and paying his fare as if he were a package being shipped.

Unfortunately, his support for air travel led to his death. He was killed in a crash, along with aviation pioneer and pilot **Wiley Post**, near Barrow, Alaska. Rogers's epitaph reads, "I never met a man I didn't like."

CLINTON RICKARD helped found the **Indian Defense League of America** (IDLA), and fought hard to preserve the sovereignty of Native American nations.

Rickard grew up on a farm in the **Tuscarora Reservation** in western New York State. When he was a young boy, his alcoholic father abused Rickard, his brothers, and his mother. Once, Rickard and his brothers hid in the outhouse from their father, who was trying to shoot them. Afterward, Rickard vowed never to drink alcohol. He later said he prayed that one day he would be able to protect others from harm.

Rickard attended school occasionally but spent most of his time working on the farm and in a local lumber mill. He completed only a third-grade education. When the **Spanish-American War** began in 1898, Rickard joined the army, partially to escape his father. The only Native American in his brigade, he served honorably, once saving his captain's life. After the war, he returned home to farm and raise a family. Rickard was married three times—his first two wives died prematurely—and he had thirteen children.

During the 1920s, Rickard became a chief of the Tuscarora and a member of their governing council. He also became interested in civil rights. Unlike such activists as **Gertrude Simmons Bonnin** (see no. 53), Rickard was strongly opposed to making Native Americans U.S. citizens. "We had our own citizenship... How can a citizen have a treaty with his own government?" he stated. He felt that the United States might be less likely to keep its treaties with Native American nations if Native Americans were U.S. citizens. (When Rickard joined the army, he felt he was following a Tuscarora tradition of fighting as allies alongside the United States.)

In 1926 Rickard helped establish the IDLA (originally the **Six Nations Defense League**). This organization provides lawyers to Native Americans who cannot afford them. It also lobbies Congress and the Canadian government to respect the civil rights of Native Americans. The IDLA achieved its first victory in 1928, when Canada and the United States agreed to respect the rights of Native Americans to freely cross the U.S.-Canada border to visit relatives and to trade.

For the next forty-five years, Rickard worked with the IDLA to preserve the sovereignty of Native American nations. He managed to obtain congressional recognition of parts of the **Jay Treaty** of 1794 and the **Treaty of Ghent** of 1814. He also worked to protect the civil liberties of Native Americans, to free from jail Native Americans who were falsely accused of crimes, and to open high schools in the state of New York to Native American students.

CHARLES ALBERT BENDER was one of the greatest baseball pitchers of the twentieth century, and the first Native American to be inducted into the **Baseball Hall of Fame**.

A member of the **Ojibwa**, Bender was born and raised in Brainerd, Minnesota, one of thirteen children. He spent his early childhood on the White Earth Chippewa Indian Reservation, but, like many Native American children of his generation, he was sent to boarding school. He attended Pennsylvania's **Carlisle Indian Industrial School**, and while there, he played on the baseball, football, basketball, and track teams. In college, he played baseball and football.

In 1902 a scout for professional baseball's **Philadelphia Athletics** discovered him while he was pitching for the Harrisburg Athletic Club, a semipro organization. Athletics manager **Connie Mack**—who was also part owner of the franchise—quickly offered him a contract. Bender played for the A's for the next twelve years.

Pitching for the A's, Bender became a sports legend. He created a special pitch, still used by pitchers today, called a slider or "nickel curve." It has been described as halfway between a fastball and a curveball. Mack quickly learned that Bender was the pitcher he needed for "must win" games. **Ty Cobb** called him "the smartest pitcher I ever faced."

Bender helped lead the A's to five World Series appearances and three world championships. His best year was 1910, when his winning percentage was .821, with a 23–5 record and a 1.58 ERA. In a career that spanned fifteen years, Bender won 210 games, while losing only 127, for a winning percentage of .623. He also won another six games in his five World Series appearances.

As one of the first Native Americans to

play major league baseball, Bender endured racial taunts and stereotyping on a regular basis. The fans nicknamed him "Chief" Bender, although he was not an Ojibwa chief. He didn't care for the nickname and always signed his autographs with his own name. When people jeered at him, doing "war whoops," Bender would shout back, "Foreigners!"

In 1914 the Baltimore Terrapins, a team in the new **Federal League**, offered Bender and some other A's players more money if they would "jump" out of the established major leagues. Bender agreed, and his last season was marred by Mack's suspicions that he was about to leave the team. After one season with the Terrapins, Bender returned to the majors in 1916 and played for the **Philadelphia Phillies** for two seasons. After he retired, he coached for several teams, including the A's.

Bender was elected to the Baseball Hall of Fame in 1953. He died of cancer the following year.

MARIA MARTINEZ was probably the most famous Native American potter of the twentieth century. Like **Nampeyo** (see no. 49), she revitalized the **Pueblo** economy in her community and transformed pottery making from a craft into an art.

Martinez was born in San Ildefonso Pueblo, a **Tewa** farming town in New Mexico. When she was around seven years old, her aunt taught her to make pottery. Like Nampeyo, Martinez was fortunate to have the chance to learn this skill, because Pueblo were beginning to use metal pots. By the time she was thirteen, Martinez was a skillful potter.

As a young woman, Maria married an old friend, **Julian Martinez**; for the rest of his life, in addition to working at other jobs, Julian collaborated with Maria to make pottery. In 1907 he helped Smithsonian Institution archaeologists excavate an ancient Pueblo ruin. One of the archaeologists asked Maria to try to duplicate the ancient Pueblo pots, using broken shards as a guide. The shards were thinner than the pots Maria usually made. Experimenting, she discovered that she could make equally thin pots if she mixed the clay with a very fine sand.

From 1909 to 1912, Maria and Julian demonstrated pottery making at the **Museum of New Mexico**. Maria would shape the pots, and Julian would paint them. They studied the museum's artifacts, trying to duplicate the black ones, and discovered that they could blacken pots with smoke.

By 1919 Julian had begun to paint the pots with white paint before they were fired, creating designs that also appeared in black but with a matte texture. These were the pots that would make Maria famous; however, at first she hid them under the bed, embarrassed that they did not look like the multicolored pots people in her community had been creating for years.

Traditionally, Pueblo potters did not sign their work, because they did not approve of calling attention to individual accomplishments. However, Martinez's customers begged her to sign her pots so they could prove they were authentic; in the 1920s she became the first Pueblo potter ever to sign her pots. In keeping with the Pueblo emphasis on the good of the community, she often gave her profits away to those in need, and she also taught other potters to make the black-on-black pots.

In 1943 Julian Martinez died, and Martinez's daughter-in-law, **Santana**, began painting her pots for her. Then in 1956, Martinez began to collaborate with her grandson, **Popovi Da**. She continued to teach and collaborate with others until her death in 1980.

Martinez received many national and international awards for her work, including several honorary doctoral degrees. Today, her pots sell for as much as $20,000.

◆ **CLARENCE TINKER** became the highest-ranking Native American officer in U.S. military history. A World War I hero, he commanded the **Seventh Air Force** in Hawaii during World War II, until he was shot down in the **Battle of Midway**.

Tinker was only one-eighth **Osage,** the son of a part-Osage man, George Ed Tinker, and a non-Osage woman, Sarah A. Tinker. However, he was raised as a member of the Osage nation in Oklahoma.

As a young man, he worked on his father's newspaper, the *Wah-Sha-She News*. He attended an Osage boarding school as a child and later attended another school for Native Americans, the **Haskell Institute** in Lawrence, Kansas. The school that probably had the greatest influence on his later career, though, was **Wentworth Military Academy**, in Lexington, Missouri.

In 1908 Tinker was commissioned as a second lieutenant in the Philippine police force. He served in the Philippines for five years. (At the time, the Philippines were being governed by the United States. Officers in the **Philippine Constabulary**, or the police force, were originally drawn from the U.S. military.) Then Tinker became a lieutenant in the U.S. Army, serving in Hawaii.

After serving in World War I, he became interested in the new, and rapidly developing, technology of flying.

Tinker entered the Air Service, became a pilot, and in 1927 was named commandant of the **Air Service Advanced Flying School**. During the 1930s he commanded several pursuit and bombardment units and air bases. At one point, on duty in London, he received the Soldier's Medal for rescuing a pilot from a crash scene. In 1940 he became a brigadier general. In December 1941, Japan bombed U.S. forces at Pearl Harbor, and Tinker was placed in charge of reorganizing Hawaii's air defenses.

Meanwhile, Native Americans were enlisting in the armed forces in great numbers. In World War II, 44,000 Native Americans served, fighting on all fronts. According to army historians, no other group made a greater per capita contribution to the war effort.

Many Native Americans became war heroes, including Clarence Tinker. In 1942 he was promoted to major general. The same year he chose to lead a bomber squadron against the retreating Japanese navy during the **Battle of Midway**. His plane was fired upon and plunged into the ocean, killing Tinker and the eight others on board. Tinker's body was never found. He was survived by his wife, daughter, and two sons. A few months later, **Tinker Air Force Base**, in Oklahoma City, Oklahoma, was named in his honor.

JIM THORPE is considered by many people to be the best all-around athlete of the first half of the twentieth century. He excelled at every sport he ever tried, and he made sports history at the **1912 Stockholm Olympics**.

A member of the **Sauk-Fox** nation, Thorpe was the great-grandson of **Black Hawk** (see no. 13). He grew up in Oklahoma, where Black Hawk's descendants were moved after they were ousted from their land in Illinois and Iowa. As a child, Thorpe attended first a mission school, and then **Haskell Institute** in Lawrence, Kansas. Then he enrolled at **Carlisle Indian Industrial School**, a famous vocational school for Native Americans in Pennsylvania. It was at Carlisle that Thorpe began his athletic career.

While there, he lettered in ten sports: football, baseball, track, boxing, wrestling, lacrosse, gymnastics, swimming, hockey, and basketball. He also won prizes for his marksmanship and, in his spare time, played golf. In 1911 and 1912, Thorpe was an all–American football player, helping Carlisle defeat some of the best college teams of those years: Harvard, Army, and Pennsylvania.

In the summer of 1912, Thorpe headed to Stockholm, Sweden, with the U.S. Olympic team. His performance at the Olympics was historic. He won both the **pentathlon** and the **decathlon**, winning the decathlon with a score almost seven hundred points ahead of the second-place finisher. It was to be thirty-six years before another Olympic athlete performed as well in the decathlon.

Unfortunately, a few months later, the Olympic Committee took Thorpe's medals back, because he had played professional minor league baseball during summers off from Carlisle. The decision was always controversial, with many people feeling that Thorpe had been penalized unfairly for a minor infraction. In 1982 the **International Olympic Committee** finally restored his records and medals.

Returning home, Thorpe became a professional football and baseball player, helping make football a popular American sport. He played for the **Canton Bulldogs**, the team that won the title of "world champion" in 1916, 1917, and 1919. In 1920 Thorpe became the first president of the **American Professional Football Association**. Two years later, it became the **National Football League**. He also founded and played on an all–Native American team, the **Oorang Indians**.

After retiring from sports, Thorpe worked at various jobs, including managing recreation for the Chicago Park System, lecturing on sports and Native American issues, and sailing with the Merchant Marine.

In 1950 sportswriters and broadcasters for the **Associated Press** named Thorpe "the greatest American football player" and the "greatest overall male athlete" for the first half of the twentieth century. Three years later, he died of a heart attack.

A linguist, ethnologist, and novelist, **ELLA CARA DELORIA** was determined not to see **Sioux** language and culture disappear like those of so many other Native American nations.

Deloria was the daughter of **Philip Deloria**, one of the first Sioux to become an **Episcopal** priest. Her parents raised her as both a Sioux and a **Christian**. As a child, she attended the Standing Rock Reservation mission school, and the All Saints School in Sioux Falls, South Dakota. A good student, she won a scholarship to Oberlin College. After two years at Oberlin, she transferred to **Columbia University**.

At Columbia, Deloria assisted **Franz Boas**, a scholar who is known as the "father of modern anthropology." Boas paid her $18 a month to translate Lakota Sioux texts. After Deloria graduated in 1915, she returned home to care for her sick mother and aging father. After her mother died, her sister, **Susan**, developed benign brain tumors that caused her to have major health problems. Deloria took care of Susan for the rest of Susan's life, a situation that made it even more difficult for her to pursue her scholarship.

In 1927 Deloria began working for Boas again, translating Sioux texts and doing fieldwork. She interviewed Sioux elders, recording Sioux stories, history, and customs. Deloria had never studied anthropology and did not consider herself an anthropologist. However, she felt a personal mission to document Sioux culture.

It was not an easy way to make a living. Deloria was always short of money and had to sell some of her family's land to pay her expenses. For a while, she and her sister Susan had to live out of her car while she conducted her fieldwork.

After several years, Deloria published *Dakota Texts*, a book of traditional Sioux stories. Nine years later, she coauthored *Dakota Grammar* with Franz Boas. Both books are still used by linguists and anthropologists today. She also wrote a book about Sioux culture, *Speaking of Indians*. Deloria managed to amass the largest body of information ever compiled about any Plains nation.

Deloria also wrote a novel, *Waterlily*. The story of the life of a Sioux woman, the book explained details of Sioux women's lives that male anthropologists at the time never bothered to study. Publishers refused to publish it, however, saying that no one would want to read about a Native American woman.

Deloria continued to research Sioux culture until she died of pneumonia in 1971. At the time of her death, she was working on a Sioux dictionary. The University of Nebraska Press finally published *Waterlily* in 1988. Largely because of Deloria's work, Sioux language and culture are better documented than those of almost any other Native American nation.

LUCY LEWIS was one of the Southwest's most famous potters. As a child, she made ashtrays that sold for a few cents each. Much later in life, she began making carefully crafted pots that became recognized nationally and internationally as important works of art.

Lewis grew up on a mesa at **Acoma Pueblo**, New Mexico. When she was seven or eight years old, her aunt taught her to make pottery. She made pots to sell to tourists, and then she rode on horseback with her mother to a train station seventeen miles away, where she could sell the pots for five or ten cents each.

Lewis married during her teen years and continued to make pots for tourists to supplement her family income. As the years progressed, she had very little spare time; her days were filled with planting gardens, raising livestock, and caring for her nine children. When she had time for pottery making, she worked as fast as she could in order to maximize her profits, sometimes painting more than a hundred pots a day.

Later, Lewis began to craft her pots much more carefully. She still made pots to sell to tourists, decorated with popular bird and flower designs. However, sometimes she painted designs of her own, inspired by shards of ancient pots she found in the dust on the mesa. She developed fine-line designs in which an outline is filled in with parallel lines.

In 1950, Lewis broke with Acoma tradition by exhibiting a fine-line pot in the **Gallup Intertribal Ceremonial** in Gallup, New Mexico. (It was against Pueblo custom for an individual to call attention to herself or her own work.) Lewis's pot won a blue ribbon, and art lovers began to collect her creations. Lewis had always signed her pots simply "Acoma Pueblo," but now she began to sign her name as well.

Although Lewis's fame was nontraditional for a Pueblo, she used only traditional methods to make her pots. She prospected the clay, ground it, and mixed sand into it. Unlike **Nampeyo** (see no. 49) and **Maria Martinez** (see no. 57), Lewis did not study pots found at archaeological sites or displayed in museums. Her creations were based simply on ancient shards she found and on her own imagination. Lewis was known for several innovations in pottery making: her fine-line technique, her use of the Zuni heart-line deer, and her use of empty space. For example, she would add dramatic effects, such as a small black figure, or black geometric shapes placed asymmetrically, to a white background.

Lewis continued to make pottery until she died in 1992.

BEN REIFEL is best remembered for being the first member of the **Sioux** nation to be elected to **Congress**. However, he dedicated much of his adult life to public service, working to improve the lives of Native Americans.

The son of a Brulé Sioux mother and a German American father, Reifel was born on South Dakota's Rosebud Reservation. Reifel's mother encouraged him to pursue an education, but his father wanted him to stay at home and work on the farm. As a result, Reifel did not finish the eighth grade until he was sixteen. His father would not allow him to go to high school, but Reifel was determined; so he ran away and enrolled in a high school 250 miles from home. After graduation, he attended South Dakota State University, earning a degree in chemistry and dairy science in 1932.

In 1933 Reifel served as a farm extension agent for the **Pine Ridge Reservation**, and in 1935 he worked to help the Sioux improve their business skills. While he was in college, Reifel had joined the U.S. Army Reserve, and during World War II he was called to duty. He served from 1942 to 1946. Before and after the war, he worked for the **Bureau of Indian Affairs** (BIA).

Following the war, he became the superintendent for the **Fort Berthold Reservation**. After receiving a scholarship to Harvard, though, he left to pursue his master's and doctoral degrees. Reifel wrote his dissertation on how to reduce conflict between Native Americans and non-Natives, a subject that was to be a project of his years later in Congress.

After completing his PhD in 1952, Reifel went back to work for the BIA. In 1954 he became the first Native American superintendent of the Pine Ridge Reservation. The following year, he became an area director for the BIA, and not long after that he ran for Congress. Reifel was elected and served for ten years.

In Congress he pushed for better education on reservations and recommended that reservation and county schools be merged so that Native Americans and non-Natives could go to school together. He also helped push through improvements to the Sioux Falls veterans' hospital and the establishment of the **National Endowment for the Humanities**.

After retiring from Congress, Reifel returned to public service as the nation's last **Commissioner of Indian Affairs**, which until 1977 was the title of the head of the Bureau of Indian Affairs. The following year, the BIA was restructured to give it a stronger voice in the Department of the Interior; since then, the head of the BIA has held the title of Assistant Secretary for Indian Affairs.

Ben Reifel died of cancer in 1990.

The first Native American to receive the **Presidential Medal of Freedom, ANNIE DODGE WAUNEKA** worked tirelessly to stop the spread of tuberculosis on the **Navajo Reservation**.

The daughter of **Henry Chee Dodge** (see no. 47), Wauneka grew up on the Navajo Reservation. When she was eight years old, Dodge sent her to boarding school at **Fort Defiance,** Arizona. Soon afterward, many students died during a flu epidemic; Wauneka contracted only a mild case and recovered. Then she helped the school's only nurse care for her sick classmates. Wauneka never forgot how her classmates suffered while they were ill.

From the fifth through eleventh grade, Wauneka attended the Albuquerque Indian School. When she returned home, she told her family she was going to marry **George Wauneka**, departing from the Navajo custom of arranged marriages. However, her family did not object. The Waunekas' marital division of labor was unusual for their day. George stayed home, caring for their children—they eventually had nine—and a large herd of sheep. Annie traveled with her father, who apparently was training her to enter politics.

As she traveled, Wauneka observed that most Navajo were poor and had no electricity or running water in their homes. She also noted that diseases tended to spread rapidly on the reservation. What she learned spurred her desire to improve the living conditions of her people.

After her father died, Wauneka became the first woman elected to the **Navajo Tribal Council,** where she was to serve for nearly thirty years. She became the chair of the Council's Health and Welfare Committee.

In her role as a health advocate, Wauneka worked to eradicate tuberculosis,

a highly contagious disease. Until the 1950s, tuberculosis was the leading cause of death in Western countries, but then doctors discovered antibiotics that could be used to treat it.

Wauneka studied tuberculosis at U.S. Public Health Service laboratories and then explained the new findings to Navajo leaders, who were suspicious of Anglo doctors. Wauneka even made up Navajo words for Western medical procedures, to calm fearful patients.

Wauneka is credited with saving the lives of at least two thousand tuberculosis victims and with convincing twenty thousand Navajos to be screened for the disease. She also carried out a crusade to improve health conditions on the reservation, hosting a weekly radio show on health and sanitation.

In 1963 President **John F. Kennedy** chose Wauneka to receive the Presidential Medal of Freedom award; President Johnson presented her with the award after Kennedy was assassinated. She continued to work to improve health conditions on the reservation until her death in 1997.

ELIZABETH PERATROVICH spent much of her life working as an advocate for civil rights for **Alaska Natives** and was instrumental in the passage of Alaska's first antidiscrimination legislation.

Peratrovich's parents died when she was very young, and she was adopted, becoming **Elizabeth Wanamaker**. She grew up in southeast Alaska, and went to college in Bellingham, Washington. There, she met and married **Roy Peratrovich**.

In 1941 the Peratrovichs decided to move back to Roy's home, Klawock, Alaska. Later, they moved to **Juneau**, where they were shocked by the racist environment they found. Klawock was a small Tlingit fishing community. However, as the territorial capital and the site of a gold rush, Juneau had experienced an influx of white immigrants. Juneau businesses had posted signs reading "We Cater to Whites Only," and "No Dogs or Natives Allowed."

Both the Peratrovichs became civil rights activists. Elizabeth became president of the **Alaska Native Sisterhood (ANS)**, while Roy became president of the Alaska Native Brotherhood (ANB), organizations that advocated equal rights for Native Alaskans.

By 1945 Territorial Governor **Ernest**

Gruening and Representative **Anthony Diamond** had managed to push an antidiscrimination bill through the territorial House of Representatives. In the Senate, though, the bill faced stiff opposition. Senator **Allen Shattuck** remarked, "Who are these people, barely out of savagery, who want to associate with us whites with five thousand years of recorded civilization behind us?"

When the floor was opened to public comment, Elizabeth Peratrovich faced the mostly white, mostly male, somewhat hostile crowd. She said calmly, "I would not have expected that I, who am barely out of savagery, would have to remind gentlemen with five thousand years of civilization behind them of our Bill of Rights." She went on to describe the realities of discrimination, remaining steadfast during two hours of aggressive questioning. When Senator Shattuck called out, "Will this law eliminate discrimination?" Peratrovich countered, "Do your laws against larceny, rape, and murder prevent those crimes?"

At this, the gallery erupted with tears and applause. Senatorial opposition to the bill crumbled, and it passed eleven to five, making it illegal for Alaskan businesses to refuse equal accommodations on the basis of race. Peratrovich spent the rest of her life working on behalf of civil rights for Native Alaskans. She pushed especially hard to achieve integration in Alaska's schools, and continued to lead the ANS, becoming the representative to the **National Congress of American Indians** for both the ANB and the ANS.

Her civil rights work was done as a volunteer. She actually earned her income during most of these years working in the offices of the Territorial Treasurer and the Territorial Vocational Rehabilitation Director. Peratrovich died of cancer in 1958.

As the first **Inupiat** newspaper editor, **HOWARD ROCK** helped organize **Native Alaskan** political organizations and used his newspaper to help persuade Congress to work toward a settlement of Alaska Native land claims.

Rock was born in 1911 in Point Hope, an ancient village on the north coast of Alaska. As a young man, he studied art at the University of Washington, and then worked as an artist, carving ivory and designing jewelry. During World War II, he served in the U.S. Army Air Forces.

Rock began his career as a community activist in 1961. He and other Inupiat discovered **Project Chariot,** a plan by the U.S. Atomic Energy Commission (AEC) to detonate several atomic bombs to create an artificial harbor near **Point Hope**. The AEC had not bothered to tell the local Inupiat, but it had already scheduled the explosion to take place in 1962. Rock spearheaded opposition to Project Chariot, and because of the outcry from the Inupiat and environmental groups, the project was canceled.

Realizing the vulnerability of their land claims, Rock and other Inupiat leaders met in November 1961 and decided to create a statewide newspaper representing Alaska Natives. Rock was to be the editor. Two years later, Athabascan leaders from Alaska's interior organized their own association, the Tanana Chiefs Conference. The group mobilized to prevent the government from building a huge hydroelectric dam that would have flooded several villages.

In 1964 Rock organized a conference in Fairbanks, bringing together leaders from various Native associations. The leaders planned ways to coordinate their efforts to get legal recognition for Alaska Native land claims, and in 1966 they decided to form an umbrella organization, the **Alaska Federation of Natives** (AFN).

In 1968 oil was discovered at **Prudhoe Bay** on Alaska's North Slope, and oil companies planned to build a pipeline from the Arctic Ocean to Prince William Sound. The AFN realized that the time had come to settle their land claims. The same year, a federal study confirmed that Alaska Natives had a valid claim to Alaska lands, which they had never signed away by treaty.

The AFN convinced Secretary of the Interior **Stewart Udall** to freeze the transfer of Alaska lands until land claims were settled. For several years, the AFN worked with Congress to hammer out a land claims bill, and Rock covered each stage of the fight in the *Tundra Times*; it was work for which he was to be nominated for a **Pulitzer Prize** a few years later.

In 1971 Congress passed the **Alaska Native Claims Settlement Act** (ANCSA), creating thirteen Alaska Native regional corporations, with title to forty-four million acres of land and more than $900 million.

JAY SILVERHEELS was known to a generation of television viewers as **Tonto**, the Lone Ranger's faithful sidekick. Silverheels is also remembered as someone who worked hard to improve Hollywood's portrayal of his people, and served as a mentor to other Native American actors.

Silverheels was born **Harold Smith** on the Six Nations Reservation in Ontario, Canada. His father was a leader of the **Mohawk**, one of the nations of the Iroquois Confederacy. During the first decades of his life, Silverheels was a champion lacrosse player in Canada and won awards in several other sports as well.

In 1938, touring with Canada's national lacrosse team, Silverheels traveled to the United States. In America, he met comedian **Joe E. Brown**, who encouraged him to begin acting and paved the way for him to begin working as a stuntman. Except for a stint in the military during World War II, for the next nine years, Silverheels played minor roles in Western movies.

In 1947 Silverheels landed his first important film role, an Aztec warrior in *The Captain from Castile*. His performance attracted attention from several directors and producers. Two years later he was cast in the part of Tonto in *The Lone Ranger*, a television show based on a hit radio series. Because Tonto helped the Lone Ranger "fight for law and order in the early West," Silverheels viewed the role as a chance to depict Native Americans in a more positive way than Hollywood normally did.

Silverheels continued to act in movies during the eight years he starred in *The Lone Ranger*. He appeared in more than thirty films, portraying such notable Native Americans as **Little Crow**, **Red Cloud**, and **Geronimo**.

His performance as Geronimo in the 1950 movie *Broken Arrow* received rave reviews. Because he was most often cast as a "good guy," many people believe that Silverheels helped change public perceptions of Native Americans. As often as possible, he deliberately chose to act in movies that showed Native Americans and people of European descent living together peacefully. He also spoke out against the practice of hiring white actors to play Native Americans.

During the 1960s, Silverheels founded the **Indian Actors Workshop**. He acted as a mentor to other Native American actors, helping them advance their careers. He also worked on public service projects intended to decrease substance abuse and help the elderly.

In the course of his life, Silverheels made nearly sixty movies. In 1979 he became the first Native American to have a star placed on Hollywood's Walk of Fame. A year later, he died of pneumonia, and his ashes were scattered on the Six Nations Reservation in Canada.

◆ **OSCAR HOWE** was one of the first Native American artists to combine traditional and modern elements in his work.

Howe, who was born on South Dakota's **Crow Creek Reservation**, had a difficult childhood. Although his great-grandfather was a tribal historian who painted Sioux history on buffalo hides, Howe's parents discouraged him from drawing. However, around the age of six, he developed a skin disease that caused open sores on his body. Other children did not want to play with him, and he spent much of his time alone, drawing.

When he turned seven, Howe was sent to the government Indian school in Pierre. He could not speak English and was often punished for speaking Sioux. His skin disease worsened, and he developed an eye disease as well. During this period, Howe's mother died. Miserable, he tried many times to run away from the school. Fortunately, school authorities decided to send him home because of his health problems, and Howe's grandmother took charge of his education for a while. She taught him about the traditional art of the **Dakota Sioux**. Eventually Howe returned to the school in Pierre, graduated from eighth grade at the age of eighteen, and began working as a laborer.

By the age of twenty, Howe had contracted tuberculosis. Told to move to a dry climate, he traveled to Santa Fe, New Mexico, to attend high school and study art. By the time he finished high school—and recovered from his illness—his paintings were being exhibited across the United States and Europe.

After serving in the army in World War II, Howe became an artist-in-residence at **Dakota Wesleyan University**, where he earned his bachelor's degree. He then completed a master's in fine arts at the University of Oklahoma and accepted a job teaching at the University of South Dakota (USD).

At USD, Howe continued to paint. He combined the ideas of abstract art, cubism, and traditional Sioux art. However, art dealers and critics often rejected his art for "not looking Indian." The final straw for Howe came in 1958, when the Philbrook Indian Art Annual committee rejected a painting of his as "a fine painting—but not Indian."

Howe wrote an angry letter in response, stating, "Whoever said that my paintings are not in the traditional Indian style has poor knowledge of Indian art indeed. There is much more to Indian art than pretty, stylized pictures..."

Howe's letter convinced the committee, and his paintings have convinced much of the art world as well. He paved the way for Native American artists who followed him to develop a variety of styles in their artwork.

PABLITA VELARDE was a painter who became one of the most influential Native American artists of the twentieth century.

Velarde grew up at **Santa Clara Pueblo**, south of Santa Fe, New Mexico. When she was three years old, her mother died of tuberculosis. Soon afterward, she was blinded by an eye infection. Her father treated her with herbs, and after two years, Velarde regained her sight. From then on she was hungry for visual details. "I wanted to see everything," she said later.

At the age of six, Velarde was sent to boarding school in Santa Fe. During the summers, she returned home, where her father and grandmother provided her with a Pueblo education. When she turned fourteen, she entered the **Santa Fe Indian School**.

Previously, the school had discouraged Native American students from painting, but at about this time, the policy was changed. The school hired a famous art teacher, **Dorothy Dunn**, and Velarde became her only female student. The boys in the classes ridiculed her, telling her to go to work in the school kitchen, because among the Pueblo, painting was traditionally a male activity.

Velarde persevered, however, inspired partly by a visit from another Pueblo woman painter, **Tonita Peña**. When Velarde had been painting for only a year, her work was exhibited at the **Museum of New Mexico**. In 1933 Santa Fe artist **Olive Rush** invited her to help paint a mural for the **Works Progress Administration** (WPA), the federal government program that created jobs through public works projects during the Depression.

In 1936 Velarde graduated and began teaching and painting in Santa Clara. She also briefly worked as a nanny for Edward Thompson Seton, the founder of the Boy Scouts. This job gave her the opportunity to travel and to exhibit and sell some of her paintings.

In 1938 the **U.S. Park Service** commissioned her to do a series of murals about Pueblo life. First, Velarde interviewed elders and researched Pueblo history. She then painted murals containing so much detailed information that today they serve as archaeological sources for scholars.

At first Velarde used casein and tempura paints in her work. Later she developed her own series of "earth colors," which she made herself by grinding rocks into powder and then mixing them with water and glue. Using these paints, Velarde was able to paint textured pictures like those often found on the walls of ancient Pueblo kivas, the underground rooms used for special ceremonies.

Velarde's work won many awards and made her internationally famous. She also paved the way for other Pueblo women—including her own daughter, **Helen Hardin**—to become artists.

IRA HAYES is best known as one of the **U.S. Marines** who raised the American flag over **Iwo Jima**, an act of bravery captured in one of the most famous photographs of **World War II**.

Hayes was born on the **Pima Reservation** in Arizona. Little is known of his early life. However, when World War II began, Hayes, along with many thousands of other Native Americans, enlisted in the armed forces.

Hayes was trained as a paratrooper and served in several battles in the Pacific. In 1945 his division landed on Iwo Jima, a Japanese island that the United States hoped to use as a base for its fighter planes. Although the navy and air force tried to weaken Japanese resistance for weeks before the marines landed, Japanese soldiers fought vigorously, and the struggle to capture Iwo Jima lasted nearly a month.

Mount Suribachi, an extinct volcano, proved to be one of the hardest areas to conquer. Hayes and the others in his division fought for each foot that they advanced. When they finally reached the peak on February 23, 1945, Hayes and five others erected an American flag as a symbol of their victory, although Iwo Jima itself had not yet been captured. A photographer named **Joe Rosenthal** captured the scene with a camera, and the resulting picture made Hayes and the others national heroes in the United States.

Only Hayes and two others in the picture survived Iwo Jima; the three of them were flown home and welcomed by President **Franklin D. Roosevelt.** Then they were given noncombat status and assigned to sell war bonds. Everywhere they went, they were honored with parades, receptions, and often, free alcohol. The constant adulation disturbed Hayes, who believed he had done no more for the United States than had any other soldier. Once, he said he wished "that guy had never made that picture."

Hayes requested permission to return to combat, but the war was nearly over. He finished his tour of duty with the marines and then went home to the Pima Reservation. But his celebrity made him feel out of place. He started to move around the country, taking jobs that never lasted very long. Everywhere he went, people offered Hayes free drinks in honor of his war service, and he rarely refused them. Eventually he became an alcoholic.

Over a period of thirteen years, Hayes was arrested more than fifty times, always for drinking-related offenses that usually began with well-wishers pressing him to accept free drinks. Finally, after his last drinking binge, Hayes passed out and died of exposure in the Arizona desert. He was remembered as "a hero to everyone but himself."

BETTY MAE TIGER JUMPER became the first **Seminole** woman, and the first Native American woman in North America, to be the leader of her nation.

Jumper began overcoming adversity as a child. At the time, some Seminole in her community made a practice of drowning babies of mixed heritage at birth, and Jumper was the daughter of a Seminole mother and white father. Her family chose not to drown her or her younger brother, but when she was five years old, a group of Seminole men came to her home and demanded that she and her then two-year-old brother be killed. However, her great-uncle, who was a Seminole religious leader, drove them away.

Soon afterward, for safety's sake, the family moved from their home in Indiantown near Lake Okeechobee to Dania Indian Reservation near Fort Lauderdale. Her mother became a fieldworker, picking beans and tomatoes, and Jumper and her brother helped.

The Seminole were determined to avoid being assimilated into mainstream U.S. culture, and they deliberately avoided white schools. Jumper's grandparents discouraged her from learning to read. One day, however, Jumper found a comic book at church—her family had been the first Seminole converts to **Christianity**—and she became determined to attend school.

At the age of fourteen, Jumper persuaded her family to let her attend a boarding school for Native Americans, nearly a thousand miles away in North Carolina. Eight years later, she and her cousin became the first Seminole to graduate from high school.

Jumper was not finished with her education, though. Recalling how frequently Seminole children died of treatable diseases like whooping cough, she moved to Oklahoma and went to nursing school. She became the first Seminole nurse and, like **Annie Dodge Wauneka** (see no. 63), worked tirelessly to improve health conditions on reservations.

In 1957 the Seminole nation put together a charter formally establishing its status as a political authority. Jumper was elected as a representative to the **Seminole Tribal Council** in the first formal election. She continued to work on the council throughout the 1960s, eventually being elected as its chairperson. As a politician, Jumper worked to improve the health, education, and housing of Seminole. She also became a founding member of the **United South and Eastern Tribes** (USET), a regional network including the Seminole, Cherokee, Choctaw, and other nations.

Jumper left office in 1971 and became the director for **Seminole Communications**, which publishes the *Seminole Tribune*. She has also narrated stories at cultural events and folklore festivals, and in the 1990s produced a video depicting several Seminole stories. In 1995 she was inducted into the **Florida Women's Hall of Fame**. She published her memoir, *A Seminole Legend*, in 2001.

DAVID SOHAPPY, a **Yakama** fisherman, was an important figure in the struggle to maintain the fishing rights of Native Americans in the Northwest.

Sohappy was the grandson of **Smohalla**, a Wanapam prophet who founded the **Dreamers** religion. Dreamers try to follow ancient practices and avoid being corrupted by European American culture. Dreamers also believe that the earth provides everything they need to live, especially salmon.

Sohappy, a Dreamer himself, attended school only through fourth grade, because his family believed reading and writing were the only useful things one could learn in a white school. As a young man, he served in the U.S. Army during World War II; after his discharge, he worked in a sawmill for a while. When he was laid off, he and his family moved to **Cook's Landing**, Washington, a temporary fishing camp alongside the **Columbia River**.

At Cook's Landing, Sohappy built a longhouse and fishing traps. The Yakama had lived along the Columbia River for thousands of years, and many families there refused to go to reservations. As a matter of religion and law, Sohappy maintained that the Yakama had the right to live next to the Columbia and fish there. In fact, an 1855 treaty guaranteed the Yakama and other nations that right.

However, the Cook's Landing camp had been created, when in order to make a dam, the government flooded Celilo, a Native village that had been protected under the 1855 treaty.

In 1968 state and federal fish and game officials raided Sohappy's home and arrested him for illegal fishing. He then took his case, *Sohappy v. Smith*, to court, resulting in a landmark U.S. District Court ruling that the 1855 treaty rights were still valid. The judge stated that Native Americans had the right to a "fair and equitable" share of the fish, and later rulings established that meant 50 percent of Columbia River salmon.

State officials disagreed. Over the next twenty years, they confiscated 230 of Sohappy's nets and often tried to evict his family from their home. In 1983 federal officials trapped Sohappy and his son in a sting operation called **Salmonscam**. Both were arrested, convicted of selling fish out of season, and sent to a federal prison to serve five years. After a public outcry, Sohappy's lawyer was able to get his case retried in tribal court, and Sohappy was released after twenty months.

However, Sohappy had suffered several strokes in prison, and his health was failing. Returning home to find another eviction notice tacked to his door, Sohappy went back to court and won his last case. He moved to a nursing home in Hood River, Oregon, where he died in 1991.

Ballet aficionados consider **MARIA TALLCHIEF** to be the first and one of the greatest **prima ballerinas** produced by the United States. She was the first American ballerina to become internationally famous.

Tallchief was the daughter of an **Osage** father and a Dutch, Scottish, and Irish mother. About twenty years before she was born, oil was discovered on Oklahoma's Osage Reservation. Many Osage, including Tallchief's family, became wealthy leasing their land to oil-drilling companies. Consequently, Tallchief's parents could afford to provide their daughters with music and dance lessons from the time they were toddlers. Tallchief, who was called Betty Marie as a child, could play the piano and had mastered ballet positions by the time she was four years old.

When Tallchief was eight, she and her family moved to Beverly Hills, California. In addition to dancing, she also began to study music and considered becoming a concert pianist. However, as a teenager, she decided to concentrate on ballet instead.

In 1942 she joined the **Ballet Russe de Monte Carlo**. The company asked her to change her name to "Tallchieva," to make her sound Russian; at the time, many ballet fans believed only Russians and Europeans could dance well. She refused but did change her first name to Maria.

George Balanchine, who was to become the most important ballet choreographer in the United States in the twentieth century, took over the troupe in 1944. He admired Tallchief, who danced the lead in many of his ballets. In 1946 the two were married, but the marriage lasted only a few years. The following year, Tallchief was invited to dance with the **Paris Opera Ballet**, becoming the first American ballerina to dance there in 108 years. There, some European reporters gossiped that she must really be French or Russian. Others imagined her to be an "Indian princess."

Upon leaving Paris, Tallchief joined Balanchine's new company—the **New York City Ballet.** Balanchine choreographed his ballets to showcase Tallchief's speed and athleticism. After she danced the lead in *Firebird*, critics described her as having an "almost frightening technical range," and her success made her internationally famous. In the following years, she danced many of her most famous roles: *Swan Lake, Serenade, Scotch Symphony*, and *The Nutcracker*. In 1953 the Osage Tribal Council honored her, and the Oklahoma State Senate declared June 29 "Maria Tallchief Day."

In her later years, Tallchief directed a corps of dancers for the **Lyric Opera of Chicago**. In 1980 she founded the **Chicago City Ballet**, which broke up nine years later. In 1996 Tallchief was awarded a **Kennedy Center Honors** award for Lifetime Achievement, the most prestigious performing arts award in the United States. She served as artistic adviser to the **Chicago Festival Ballet** from 1990 until her death in 2013.

Organizer and activist **LADONNA HARRIS** has spent her life working to protect the rights of Native Americans as well as becoming involved in the feminist and peace movements.

Harris was born in Temple, Oklahoma, to a **Comanche** mother and Irish American father. Her parents separated shortly after her birth because of the discrimination they faced as a mixed-race couple. Harris was raised by her Comanche grandparents. Her grandmother was a Christian and her grandfather was a traditional healer, but they respected each other's beliefs and raised Harris to respect the beliefs of others. Harris spoke only Comanche until she began attending public school at the age of six. She attended an integrated school, and children on the bus taunted her about being an Indian.

In high school, LaDonna met **Fred Harris**, the son of a poor white sharecropper, and the two were married soon after he entered college. LaDonna put her career on hold while she worked to support her husband's education and to bring up their three children. After Fred became a U.S. senator from Oklahoma, LaDonna began to pursue her own interests.

In 1965, at a time when the country was caught up in the African American civil rights movement, Harris was working to end segregation of Native Americans in Oklahoma. She worked with sixty of the state's Native nations, and organized Oklahoma's first intertribal organization, **Oklahomans for Indian Opportunity**.

By this time, Harris had become a nationally known activist. In 1967 President **Lyndon Johnson** appointed her chairperson of the National Women's Advisory Council of the War on Poverty; later he appointed her to the **National Council on Indian Opportunity** (NCIO), a council he created.

When Richard Nixon became president in 1969, he placed the NCIO on the back burner, and Harris resigned. She then helped found the **National Women's Political Caucus**. In 1970 she founded **Americans for Indian Opportunity (AIO)** and became its first president. AIO works to strengthen tribal governments. It also created a national computer network called INDIANnet, a resource dedicated to making the internet accessible to Native Americans.

Harris soon also became an important peace activist. President Jimmy Carter encouraged her to form a Native American version of the Peace Corps, called the **Peace Pipe Project**. She found that indigenous people in other countries felt comfortable working with indigenous people from the Americas, and the Peace Pipe workers learned skills that helped them find better jobs when they returned to the United States.

At the turn of the twenty-first century, Harris continued to work with the AIO and also served on the boards of many nonprofit organizations. In 2017 she was an honorary cochair of the Women's March on Washington, and in 2018 she was included in the first group of inductees to the National Native American Hall of Fame.

LOUIS BALLARD was one of the most popular contemporary Native American composers. His work is performed by philharmonic orchestras and ballet companies across the United States and Europe.

Ballard was born in northeast Oklahoma, the son of a **Quapaw French** mother and a **Cherokee Scot** father. During his youth, he spent time both on the reservation, visiting his grandmother, and in European American communities, with his mother and stepfather. In both environments, music surrounded him.

At tribal ceremonials, Ballard learned Quapaw songs and dances; his mother, a pianist, wrote children's songs. Ballard's grandmother encouraged him to take piano lessons. Soon after he began to learn the piano, Ballard started to compose his own music. He also grew interested in the music of other Native American nations.

As a young adult, Ballard studied music at the University of Tulsa, where he earned a bachelor's degree. To finance his education, he worked as a janitor, dishwasher, ambulance driver, and waiter, as well as a nightclub pianist and singer. The focus of Ballard's early formal musical training was classical music, and he especially admired the Hungarian composer **Béla Bartók**.

Bartók incorporated Hungarian folk music into his compositions, and Ballard was inspired to incorporate Native American themes into his own work. Many European composers had written instrumental works based on their perception of Native Americans, but Ballard felt these works to be inauthentic. He believed classical composers could learn from and incorporate Native American harmonies and instruments.

To this end, Ballard began collecting music from many Native American traditions. Determined to bring Native music into the mainstream, he composed ballets, chamber music, orchestral variations, and choral arrangements inspired by Native music and using Native American instruments.

In 1960 he wrote a ballet, *Koshare*, based on a **Hopi** creation story. In 1969 he won an award for his woodwind quartet *Ritmo Indio*, which replaces the usual oboe with a Lakota instrument similar to a flute. Ballard has also written works based on historical incidents or real people, such as *Incident at Wounded Knee*, and *Portrait of Will Rogers*, a cantata based on the life of Will Rogers. Symphony orchestras, ballet companies, and choirs have performed his works frequently.

In addition to composing his own music, Ballard worked to bring Native American music to young music students across the country. In the 1970s, he served as dean of the music department for the **Institute of American Indian Arts** in Santa Fe, New Mexico, and as the music curriculum specialist for the **Bureau of Indian Affairs**. Over the years, he also worked with reservation schools to make it possible for students to use Native instruments and learn the cultural context for Native American music.

The first **Navajo** ever to earn a PhD in physics, **FRED BEGAY** won many awards for his service to the Navajo nation and for mentoring young minority science students.

Begay was born at Towaoc, Colorado, on the Ute Mountain Indian Reservation. His parents, who were both Navajo and Ute, were traditional Navajo healers. Begay grew up speaking both Navajo and **Ute**. When he was six years old, his parents began training him to practice Navajo medicine, starting with the songs of the Blessing Way ceremony.

When he was ten, he began to attend a Bureau of Indian Affairs boarding school. Like most of these schools, the one Begay attended prohibited students from speaking their own languages or attending Native American religious ceremonies. The school trained students to become farmers. "They thought we weren't intelligent enough for academic learning," Begay remembered.

When he was nineteen, having still not graduated from high school, Begay joined the U.S. Army Air Corps and served in the Korean War. Returning home, he married

and set about raising children and running a farm. But the Navajo nation was recruiting war veterans to go to college. Begay enrolled at the University of New Mexico, which accepted him with the understanding that he would also complete his high school diploma (he didn't). Sixteen years, seven children, and a doctorate in nuclear physics later, he was offered a job at **Los Alamos National Laboratory**.

Many people later asked Begay how he was able to complete a doctorate in nuclear physics without having ever finished high school. The answer he gave is that his early Navajo math and science training served him well. Navajo math uses base-8 arithmetic, just like computer science and fractal geometry. Navajo weavers use complex geometrical designs in their weaving, and Navajo science includes versions of the concepts of gravity, fusion energy, solar radiation, and even the modern gas discharge laser.

Although Los Alamos is famous as the place where the first atom bomb was developed, Begay's work was in other areas. One of his goals was to find an alternative energy source, joining atoms to give off heat. In addition to his work at Los Alamos, he frequently advised the Navajo nation about science and technology and even taught science classes to middle school Navajo students.

In 1999 Begay won the **Distinguished Scientist Award** from the Society for Advancement of Chicanos/Hispanics and Native Americans in Science. He also headed the **Seaborg Hall of Science**, an organization that provides science- and technology-related services, especially education, to the Navajo community.

In 1992 **Northern Cheyenne** chief **BEN NIGHTHORSE CAMPBELL** became the first Native American to serve in the **U.S. Senate** in more than sixty years.

Campbell had a very difficult upbringing; his father was an alcoholic, and his mother suffered from tuberculosis. He and his sister sometimes lived in orphanages and briefly with their mother in a sanitarium, where she had been institutionalized for her health. The family was very poor. Campbell recalled one evening when his mother opened a can of peas, gave the peas to the kids, and then drank the juice for her own dinner. When he was growing up, Campbell later remarked, "becoming a U.S. senator was just about the last thing I imagined."

Like many kids who grow up in rough circumstances, Campbell dropped out of school. He joined the air force and served in the Korean War while completing a GED high school certificate. He later said that the military gave his life predictability, structure, and a regular income—three things that had been lacking during his youth. Campbell turned to sports as an escape. He studied martial arts, becoming one of the youngest Americans to hold a fourth-degree black belt in judo. In 1964 he captained the U.S. judo team at the Summer Olympics in Tokyo.

When he returned from Korea, Campbell attended San Jose State University, where he studied physical education and fine arts. Later he attended Meiji University in Tokyo. He also began to work as a jewelry designer, using the name Ben Nighthorse; his designs have won more than two hundred awards.

In 1982 Campbell entered politics and was elected to the Colorado State Legislature. In 1987 he moved on to the **U.S. House of Representatives**, becoming, as he said, "the only member of Congress who goes to work on a motorcycle." In 1992

he decided to run for the Senate and won. There, he became the first Native American ever to chair the Senate's **Indian Affairs Committee**.

Campbell also served on other important committees related to energy and natural resource management. He has worked hard to pass legislation settling Native American water rights and protecting Colorado's wilderness areas. In addition, he has led the battle to prevent **fetal alcohol syndrome**, the birth defects that afflict babies born to mothers who drink alcohol during pregnancy.

In 1995 Campbell shocked political observers by switching from the Democratic to the Republican Party. He said at the time that he felt the Democratic Party had been taken over by special interests. In 1998, running as a Republican, Campbell was reelected to another term. He retired in 2005.

Historian and activist **VINE DELORIA JR.** was one of the founders of the scholarly field of Native American studies.

Deloria was born to a distinguished **Sioux** family. His great-grandfather was a Sioux healer, and his grandfather was an Episcopal missionary. His aunt **Ella Cara Deloria** (see no. 60) was a famous ethnographer, and his father was the first Native American to be named to a national position in the Episcopal Church. As a young boy during the 1930s, Deloria grew up listening to veterans of the Battle of the Little Bighorn tell stories about that famous battle.

At first, Deloria considered following in his father's footsteps as a minister. After a brief stint in the U.S. Marine Corps (1954–1956), he earned a degree from Iowa State University and then attended Augustana Lutheran Seminary. He went on to earn a master's degree in sacred theology and began working for United Scholarship Service, a church group.

In 1959 Deloria became the executive director for the **National Congress of American Indians** (NCAI) and worked to prevent various Native nations from having their tribal recognition terminated. Deloria began to realize that many Native nations did not have lawyers. So he again returned to school, this time completing a law degree. While attending law school, he wrote his first book, *Custer Died for Your Sins*, which became known as an "Indian rights manifesto."

After completing his degree, Deloria and his family moved to Washington, where they became involved with the struggle for Puyallup and Nisqually fishing rights. He also taught college classes. Using his legal training, Deloria wrote books, such as *Of Utmost Good Faith* and *Behind the Trail of Broken Treaties*, documenting the treaties, acts, and rulings that affect Native Americans. He also helped defend **American Indian Movement** leaders during their trial for the occupation of Wounded Knee.

Deloria's books presented an activist viewpoint on Native American issues. His writing often touched upon religious themes, and his 1973 book, *God Is Red*, shocked the nation with its indictment of Christianity's role in Native American genocides. In *Red Earth, White Lies* (1995), he tried to refute the theory that Native Americans first came to the Americas via the Bering Strait land bridge 15,000 years ago by claiming that they actually lived in North America as early as 200,000 years ago.

Deloria served as a professor of political science at the University of Arizona from 1978 to 1990 and then taught at the University of Colorado Boulder until retiring in 2000.

JANET MCCLOUD helped found at least five Native American activist organizations.

A descendant of **Chief Seathl** (see no. 18), McCloud was born on Washington's Tulalip Reservation. As a child, she was left alone with her younger sisters and cousins while her alcoholic mother and stepfather went out drinking. Meanwhile, drunks from the neighborhood would come into the house and abuse her and the other children. By the time McCloud was seven years old, she had taught the older kids to defend the younger kids, using axes and knives to drive the drunks out of the house. McCloud later explained, "So, that was my first organizing."

McCloud wound up living in foster homes, developed low self-esteem, and tried to commit suicide at age twelve. She married very young and was soon divorced. Then she married **Don McCloud**. The two moved out of the city and began living off the land.

In the 1960s, McCloud hoped to organize the Tulalip and Nisqually to develop their own fisheries. However, the state of Washington did not recognize Native fishing rights guaranteed by treaties. In 1961 the state arrested several Nisqually fishermen. Authorities insisted they had the right to regulate fisheries and accused Native fishermen of depleting the salmon population by overfishing.

Along with women such as **Ramona Bennett** (see no. 85), McCloud kept a vigil in the fishing boats, in what would later be known as "fish-ins." She and her husband founded the **Survival of American Indians Association** to fight state policies, and McCloud began publishing the association's newsletter, *Survival News*. The fish-ins continued, and McCloud and her family were sometimes arrested.

When comedian Dick Gregory arrived

to support the protesters, he was arrested and began fasting in jail. McCloud then put up a tepee across from the jail and told police that because the state was not keeping treaties with Northwest Natives, she was reclaiming the land.

The fishing rights activists eventually succeeded to some extent. The courts ruled that Native Americans in Washington had a right to half of the fish caught in coastal waters.

The fish-ins were not the end of McCloud's activism, however. In the early 1970s, she worked with the Native American Rights Fund (NARF) and founded the **Brotherhood of American Prisoners**. Later she helped organize **Women of All Red Nations** (WARN), a sister group to the American Indian Movement (AIM), and the Northwest Indian Women's Circle.

McCloud also built a lodge called the **Sapa Dawn Center**, dedicated to the pursuit of justice for indigenous families. In 1985 women from several countries met there with McCloud and formed the **Indigenous Women's Network**, an organization that advocates the sovereignty of Native nations in the Americas.

NAVARRE SCOTT MOMADAY began a Native American literary renaissance in the 1960s when his book *House Made of Dawn* made him the first Native American writer to win the **Pulitzer Prize** for fiction.

A **Kiowa**, Momaday lived on the Kiowa Reservation in Oklahoma for the first two years of his life. Then his parents accepted teaching jobs on reservations in Arizona. Momaday grew up in the Southwest, exposed not only to his own Kiowa traditions but also to the Navajo, Apache, and Pueblo cultures.

Momaday's father was a painter, and his mother was a writer who loved English literature. She so influenced the imaginative young Momaday that, as a child, he thought he saw the shadow of Grendel, a monster from the epic poem *Beowulf*, on the wall of Canyon de Chelly.

For most of his childhood, Momaday attended school on reservations in Arizona and New Mexico. He also attended a Virginia military academy for a year. After graduating, he attended the University of New Mexico and then taught school for a year on the Jicarilla Apache Reservation. Then he won a fellowship to Stanford University, where he entered a doctoral program in American literature. After leaving Stanford, he taught at the University of California, Santa Barbara.

Momaday's first novel, *House Made of Dawn*, was published in 1968. The story of a Native American veteran adjusting to life after World War II, the book earned the Pulitzer Prize and made Momaday famous. The next year, he moved to the University of California at Berkeley and published *The Way to Rainy Mountain*, a work that blends memoir with folklore and that many critics have called his greatest. While at Berkeley, Momaday didn't confine himself to writing. He also designed a graduate program in **Indian Studies** and taught courses in American Indian literature and mythology.

Although Momaday is famous for his novels—his other books include *The Names* and *The Ancient Child*—he thinks of himself as more of a poet than a novelist. He published several collections of poetry, and received the **Academy of American Poets** prize in 1962 for "The Bear." In an interview, Momaday noted that people pay more attention to novels, but that he considers poetry the "highest form of expression." He expresses himself as an artist too. In 1974 he began to draw and paint, finally pursuing his father's interest in the visual arts. His works have been exhibited throughout the United States, and contemporary editions of his books often include his illustrations.

In addition to his groundbreaking Pulitzer Prize win, he received many other awards, including the first Lifetime Achievement Award from the Native Writers Circle of the Americas in 1992 and a National Medal of Arts in 2007. He also helped found **Buffalo Trust**, an organization dedicated to preserving Native culture for future generations.

Menominee activist **ADA E. DEER** led a movement to restore her people's status as a federally recognized tribe and later became the first woman to head the **Bureau of Indian Affairs** (BIA).

Deer grew up on the Menominee Reservation in northern Wisconsin. Until she turned eighteen, she lived with her family, which included her Menominee father, white mother, and four younger siblings, in a one-room log cabin with no heat or running water.

Deer's mother impressed on her at an early age that she had a duty to help her people, and it became a lifelong effort on her part. She earned a bachelor's degree in social work from the University of Wisconsin–Madison, becoming its first Menominee graduate. Then she became the first Native American to earn a master's degree in social work from Columbia University. She briefly attended the University of Wisconsin–Madison Law School, but she left to help the Menominee, whose plight was becoming urgent.

In 1954 Congress terminated the Menominee's status as a federally recognized tribe, believing they were prosperous enough to survive without federal assistance. The government schools and reservation hospital were shut down, the land became subject to taxation, and the tribal membership rolls were closed. Soon, their leaders were selling land in a desperate attempt to raise money.

In 1970 Deer joined other Menominee in forming DRUMS, **Determination of the Rights and Unity of Menominee Shareholders**. She also became the vice president of the National Committee to Save the Menominee People and Forest, and she traveled to Washington, DC, to persuade Congress to reinstate the Menominee as a tribe. In 1973 President Richard Nixon signed the **Menominee Restoration Act**; it was a historical reversal of American Indian policy and set an important precedent for other tribes.

Deer was elected chairperson of the newly formed Menominee government; after ushering through a transition period, she resigned. For fifteen years she taught at the University of Wisconsin–Madison. During the 1980s and 1990s, she returned to politics, making two unsuccessful bids for Wisconsin Secretary of State and one for Congress.

In 1993 President Bill Clinton appointed Deer to head the **Bureau of Indian Affairs**, making her the first woman assistant secretary of the Department of the Interior.

Deer worked to give Native American nations more control over the BIA funds they received, while lobbying against those in Congress who wanted to reduce the BIA budget. She left office in 1997 and returned to academia, to the University of Wisconsin–Madison, where she became the director of American Indian Studies and a distinguished lecturer at the School of Social Work.

As a cofounder of the **American Indian Movement** (AIM), **CLYDE BELLECOURT** focused on fighting for Native American rights, teaching young people about Native American history, and educating the American public about conditions on reservations.

Bellecourt grew up in Minnesota, on an **Ojibwa** reservation. His Ojibwe name is Nee-gon-we-way-we-dun, which means "Thunder Before the Storm." He dropped out of school after the ninth grade and moved to the city to try to find work; when he was unable to find a job, he began committing robberies. Eventually, he ended up in Minnesota's **Stillwater State Prison**. Depressed, Bellecourt started a hunger strike. Another inmate, **Eddie Benton Benai,** began dropping a candy bar into Bellecourt's cell every day. Bellecourt didn't touch them and the pile grew.

One day Benai brought him a book about the Ojibwa instead. This caught Bellecourt's interest. He ended his hunger strike and eventually started teaching other Native American prisoners about Native culture and history.

In 1968, along with Benai, **George Mitchell**, and **Dennis Banks** (see no. 82), Bellecourt founded AIM. At first AIM's main goal was to protect Natives in Minneapolis from police brutality. Bellecourt formed a street patrol that would monitor police calls and film arrests of Native Americans. They also informed Natives being arrested about their right to an attorney. The patrols were effective, greatly reducing the number of Natives arrested.

Next, the AIM activists put together schools for Native American children. The schools offered students an education in Native American culture and history to counteract what they claimed was the biased presentation in American history textbooks. Native American elders taught students spiritual ceremonies that had previously been outlawed.

Then AIM began to engage in what Bellecourt called "confrontational politics." In 1969 about two hundred AIM activists took over the abandoned prison on **Alcatraz Island**, in San Francisco Bay. They stated that it would be a "suitable" place for a reservation and offered to buy it for cheap jewelry worth $24—the sum for which Manhattan Island had been bought from the Indians.

In 1973 AIM members took over the village of **Wounded Knee**, causing the federal government to besiege the town. Many AIM activists at Wounded Knee armed themselves, but Bellecourt, a pacifist, refused to carry a weapon.

Like other leaders, Bellecourt was arrested and charged for his activities at Wounded Knee, but the charges were dropped. In the mid-1970s, Bellecourt returned to AIM's earlier project, founding schools. He helped found several alternative schools for Native Americans throughout the country.

In 1979 Bellecourt helped found the **American Indian Opportunities Industrial Center**, the first school in the United States to offer vocational training specifically for Native Americans. In the 1980s and 1990s, he organized several youth service centers. He also helped found several other organizations, including the Elaine M. Stately Peacemaker Center for Indian Youth, the Native American Community Clinic, Women of Nations Eagles Nest Shelter, and the Legal Rights Center.

DENNIS BANKS was one of the founders of the **American Indian Movement** (AIM), an organization that works to defend Native American civil rights.

Banks was born on the Leech Lake Reservation, an **Ojibwa** reservation in northern Minnesota. He was taken from his family at the age of five and sent to a Bureau of Indian Affairs (BIA) boarding school.

In 1953 Banks joined the air force and was sent to Japan. After he returned home, he drifted from one city to another, unable to find a job. In 1966 he went to prison for burglary. After his release, he met with **Clyde Bellecourt**, **George Mitchell,** and **Eddie Benton Banai**, ex-convicts who were concerned about the lack of jobs, education, and housing for urban Native Americans. Together they founded the American Indian Movement.

At first, Banks and Bellecourt organized street patrols, filming arrests of Native Americans and informing arrestees of their legal rights. Banks and Bellecourt were often beaten up by police and jailed. Later they put together a program for mothers of juvenile offenders to report on racism within the juvenile court system. They also worked with the public school system to get rid of racist textbooks. Then they founded schools of their own where Native students could learn about their heritage.

In the early 1970s, AIM became known for its dramatic political protests, such as the occupation of **Alcatraz** and the **Trail of Broken Treaties**, a march on Washington, DC. In 1973 Banks, Bellecourt, and other AIM activists took over the village of **Wounded Knee** and proclaimed it the "Independent Oglala Nation," partly because of Wounded Knee's historical significance, and partly because local elders had asked for their help. Soon they were surrounded by the FBI, U.S. marshals, and the BIA police. Federal officials laid siege to the village, occasionally exchanging fire with the activists. After seventy-one days of negotiations, the activists agreed to allow themselves to be arrested.

Banks was acquitted of the Wounded Knee charges but was convicted of charges stemming from an earlier protest. However, he escaped to California, where Governor **Jerry Brown** offered him amnesty. There, he began teaching. When Brown's term as governor ended, New York's Onondaga Nation offered Banks refuge. Instead, in 1984 he surrendered to authorities and served an eighteen-month prison sentence. Afterward he returned to the Pine Ridge Reservation to work as a drug and alcohol counselor.

In the late 1980s and 1990s, Banks published his autobiography, *Sacred Soul*, in Japan, and starred in several films. In 2001, at the age of sixty-nine, he returned to the Leech Lake Reservation and started his own wild rice and maple syrup company.

PETERSON ZAH led the efforts to reorganize the **Navajo** tribal government, and became the last chairman and its first elected president in 1990.

Zah grew up in Low Mountain, Arizona, in a disputed land area called the **Navajo-Hopi Joint Use Area**. Both Navajo and Hopi lived in the area, and Zah grew comfortable with both cultures.

When Zah was nine years old, he was taken from his family and sent to boarding school in Phoenix. (For years, the Bureau of Indian Affairs had a policy of separating Native American children from their families, often by force, and sending them to boarding schools where teachers tried to make them abandon their language and culture.) Several years later, he attended Phoenix College, where he played basketball and graduated in 1960. He then transferred to Arizona State University, where he graduated in 1963 with a degree in education.

In 1967 Zah moved to Window Rock, Arizona, and took the job that would be his stepping stone to politics: head of **Dinébeiina Nahiilna Be Agaditahe** (DNA). DNA provided legal assistance to Navajo—and later Hopi and Apache—whose annual income was under $3,500. Zah was involved in thousands of DNA cases, including some landmark impact decisions rendered by the U.S. Supreme Court.

Zah did not spend all of his time working for DNA—he also served on the first all-Navajo school board at Window Rock and became its president in 1973. He pushed the board to hire more Navajo teachers and to teach the Navajo language, culture, and history in the schools.

In 1978 many Navajo pressed Zah to run for tribal chairperson, but he waited until 1982 to take on incumbent **Peter MacDonald.** The Navajo-Hopi land dispute became an important issue in the campaign. In 1974 Congress had passed an act giving half the land to the Hopi and requiring many Navajo and some Hopi to relocate to other areas. Zah stressed the importance of coexistence and healing the damage done by the land dispute. He won the election and then began working with the Hopi people to resolve the land dispute and reform the tribal government. In the next election, though, he narrowly lost to MacDonald.

However, MacDonald's administration quickly fell apart. He was convicted of corruption and bribery in a tribal court, and then of conspiracy and assault in federal court, and was sent to federal prison for fourteen years. Zah ran again in 1990 and, after winning, became the first president of the Navajo Nation under the newly reorganized government structure. He held the position until 1995. That year, he became an adviser to the president on American Indian Affairs at Arizona State University.

BILLY MILLS became the first American athlete to win a gold medal in a long distance track event at the **Olympic Games**.

Mills grew up on the Lakota's Pine Ridge Reservation in South Dakota, one of eight children. His mother died when he was six years old, his father when he was twelve. After Mills's father died, he was sent to a Bureau of Indian Affairs boarding school, the Haskell Institute in Lawrence, Kansas.

As a member of the football team, Mills rejected track as a "sissy" sport. However, when he began to train in track to improve his general conditioning, he realized that it was a demanding physical discipline. He became a strong competitive runner, winning both the Kansas two-mile and one-mile championships twice in a row.

After Mills graduated from high school, the University of Kansas awarded him a full athletic scholarship. Although he became a star on the track team that won national championships twice, when he tried and failed to qualify for the 1960 Olympic team, he left college never expecting to run again competitively.

Mills joined the marines and began running again. After he won the interservice 10,000-meter race, the marines sent Mills, still an unknown athlete, to the Olympic trials for the 1964 games, and he made the U.S. team.

The odds of Mills winning a gold medal in his race, the 10,000 meter, were about 1,000 to 1. During the early stage of the race, he was pushed by other runners and dropped behind. But before long, he regained his stride, and he took the lead in the home stretch. Then he was passed by two other runners, and it seemed as if he had no chance of winning. Suddenly, he kicked in with a tremendous sprint, and regained the lead with about 80 meters to go. With the crowd roaring at the stunning developments, Mills won the race, in a time of 28:24.4. He had improved his own previous best time by nearly a minute, and set a new **Olympic record** as well.

When Mills returned home from the Olympics, the **Lakota** honored him with a ring made of gold from the Black Hills. The ring reminded Mills that those who achieve great things have a responsibility to give something back to their community. Since his Olympic triumph, he has done just that. For years, he has visited nearly every reservation and urban Native center in the United States and has traveled to more than fifty other countries to speak about Native American issues.

Mills also helped found **Running Strong for American Indian Youth**, which raises money for food, medicine, and clothing for reservations and aims to help communities establish self-sufficiency. Since his Olympic victory, he has received numerous awards and honors, including being inducted into the United States Olympic Hall of Fame in 1984 and winning the **Presidential Citizens Medal** in 2012.

Along with fellow activist **Janet McCloud** (see no. 78), **RAMONA BENNETT** played an important part in the struggle to defend the fishing rights of **Northwest Native Americans**.

Bennett grew up in Seattle and attended public school there, but she felt out of place. She was often depressed. Then, she says, her life turned around after she visited the **Seattle Indian Center** and began volunteering with the Indian Service League.

In the 1950s, Bennett moved to the Puyallup Reservation. There were few jobs, and the community was very poor. Bennett was elected to the **Puyallup Tribal Council** in the 1960s and, determined to do something about the conditions, began lobbying Congress about problems on the reservation.

"If I couldn't get an appointment with a Congressman," she later explained, "I'd wait outside his door for the bell to ring calling him to vote—and when he came out, I'd run with him." The tribal council could not often afford round-trip tickets to Washington, DC, so afterward, Bennett would sometimes hitchhike the three thousand miles home.

During the 1960s, the Puyallup depended on fishing, because few people on the reservation had jobs. However, fishing put them in conflict with state fishing conservation regulations. With Janet McCloud, Bennett helped found the **Survival of American Indians Association** to defend Native fishing rights. In 1970 the state banned fishing traps and sent law enforcement agents to stop the Puyallup from fishing. State officials took the traps and jailed the fishermen.

Bennett and others set up an armed camp on the riverbank to defend the fishermen. After ten weeks, agents raided the camp, using tear gas and clubs, arrested Bennett and the others, and charged them with incitement to riot. The protesters faced a possible thirty-five years in prison. The case was thrown out of court when the secretary of the interior stated that the agents had been trespassing on Puyallup land. Later, courts ruled that Native Americans had a right to half the fish caught in Washington coastal waters.

In 1972 Bennett was elected chairperson of the Puyallup Tribal Council. Only a few women headed tribal councils at the time, and the National Tribal Chairmen's Association tried to deny her admittance to their meeting, asking her to sit with the chairmen's wives. Bennett had to push her way in. Once she was in, she demanded that the association prioritize the needs of children.

Bennett left the tribal council after eight years as its chairperson, and began to devote herself to the needs of minority children. She became the executive director of **Rainbow Youth and Family Services**, an organization she established to help children of color resist being adopted outside their home communities.

Author and poet **PAULA GUNN ALLEN** spent much of her life trying to increase the recognition of the Native American literary tradition.

Allen described her birth as a "multicultural event." She grew up in a **Laguna Pueblo** community near Albuquerque, New Mexico, but her ancestors are Pueblo, Sioux, Lebanese, and Scottish American. She was raised mostly by her mother and grandmother and grew up taking for granted the respected place of women in Laguna Pueblo culture.

Allen said that until she became involved with the feminist movement in the 1960s and 1970s, she did not realize that women were not equally respected in the Western tradition. She remarked, "I grew up with the notion that women are strong. I didn't know that I was supposed to be silly and weak."

As a child, Allen attended mission schools, and in high school she went to a Catholic boarding school. She started college at the University of New Mexico and then transferred to the University of Oregon, where she began writing poetry. In Oregon she began to experience what writer **N. Scott Momaday** (see no. 79) calls "land-sickness"—she was so homesick for her Laguna community that she became depressed.

Reading Momaday's book *House Made of Dawn* helped her understand what was happening to her. After finishing her master's degree, Allen married and had three children. The marriage ended in divorce, and after two more failed marriages, she came to the realization that she was a lesbian.

Returning to the University of New Mexico, Allen thought she would pursue a PhD in Native American literature, but, according to her dean, Native American literature did not exist. Allen completed her degree in American studies instead and began a career as a college professor. Over the years, she has taught at the University of New Mexico; the University of California, Berkeley; and the University of California, Los Angeles.

While she was still in school, Allen published her first book of poetry and went on to publish seven other volumes of poetry after that. She also published a novel. Since then, she has written several more volumes of poetry and a novel. She also wrote two biographies and several academic books. She has worked to educate the public about Native American literature. In 1983 she edited an anthology of essays and course designs on Native American literature. She has also edited two anthologies of Native American literature, one of which, *Spider Woman's Granddaughters*, won the **American Book Award** in 1990.

Perhaps Allen is best known for her groundbreaking contribution to feminist literature, her 1986 book *The Sacred Hoop*, a study of Native traditions that center on women. She won a Lifetime Achievement Award from the **Native Writers Circle of the Americas** in 2001.

One of the founders of the **Alaska Federation of Natives**, **WILLIAM HENSLEY** was instrumental in helping convince Congress to pass the **Alaska Native Claims Settlement Act** of 1971.

Hensley was born in Kotzebue, Alaska, to an **Inupiat** family. As a child, he attended elementary school in Alaska, but then he was removed from his family and taken to a boarding school in Knoxville, Tennessee. At the time, the Bureau of Indian Affairs had a policy of removing children from their families, sometimes forcibly, and placing them in boarding schools where teachers tried to make them abandon their culture. Hensley attended several colleges before transferring to George Washington University in Washington, DC, where he graduated in 1966. Returning to Alaska, he took a course on constitutional law, and wrote a paper called, "What Rights to Land Have the Alaska Native?"

At the time, leaders of regional Native organizations were beginning to organize. Hensley mailed copies of his paper to village leaders in the Kotzebue area. As Hensley's paper was passed around, he found himself closely involved in the land claims dispute. He attended meetings with village leaders from the Kotzebue region, and in 1966 helped found the **Northwest Alaska Native Association** (NANA) to protect the interests of Alaska Natives in that area.

The same year, Hensley helped found the Alaska Federation of Natives (AFN). He became the executive director, president, and cochairman of the AFN. The organization lobbied Congress to pass the Alaska Native Claims Settlement Act of 1971, recognizing Alaska Native rights to forty-four million acres of land and providing $1 billion to organize thirteen Native corporations to manage Native money and land. NANA became one of the new Native corporations, and Hensley became its executive director and chairman.

In 1966 Hensley was elected as a representative to the **Alaska State Legislature** and in 1970 became a state senator. During his early years in the legislature, he continued to work on behalf of AFN and the land claims struggle. However, he also worked on other issues.

As senator, Hensley represented twenty thousand people living in a district that was slightly larger than the state of Montana. Few villages in that area had electricity. Hensley founded the **Alaska Village Electric Cooperative**, which shortly thereafter hooked up electricity to fifty villages that had never had it.

Hensley left office in 1974 but returned again in 1986 for two years. In 1987 he pushed the Alaska Legislature to form a committee on suicide prevention. The committee investigated the issue of suicide in rural Alaska—which has one of the highest suicide rates in the country—and formed a long-term suicide prevention program.

Poet **SIMON J. ORTIZ** was part of a trio of writers who laid the groundwork for the Native American literary renaissance of the 1960s and 1970s.

Ortiz spent his early childhood years in a small village near **Acoma Pueblo**, in New Mexico. At first he spoke only Acoma, but at his school, teachers hit students on the back or knuckles if they spoke their own language. So Ortiz learned English. He was excited about attending even such a harsh school, because he loved stories and loved learning to read.

After the sixth grade, Ortiz was sent to St. Catherine's boarding school in Santa Fe, New Mexico. Teachers there tried to convert students to Catholicism. Ortiz was disappointed, but he escaped into his books, writing in a diary, and reading anything he could find, even the dictionary. He did not consider becoming a writer, because he knew of no Native American writers. Instead, he decided to learn a trade and took classes in sheet metal and woodworking.

After graduating from high school, Ortiz began work as a laborer in the uranium industry. In 1962 he left to go to college, using a Bureau of Indian Affairs grant and his savings. At about this time, he began drinking. "No one could tell me the dangers of alcohol use," he said later, "and I was arrogant enough to think I could control it."

Frustrated by his college experience, Ortiz joined the army. He decided to return to school when he got out. He enrolled at the University of New Mexico but quit in 1968. At about this time, Ortiz became aware of Native American political activists, and was inspired by **N. Scott Momaday's** book *House Made of Dawn* (see no. 79).

In 1969 Ortiz completed a master of fine arts degree at the University of Iowa and was "discovered" by the National Endowment for the Arts, which gave him a journalism award. He began writing poetry during the 1970s, and his first book of poetry, *Going for the Rain*, came out in 1976, the same year as **Leslie Marmon Silko's** *Ceremony* (see no. 95). Together, the works of Momaday, Silko, and Ortiz marked a new period of Native American literature.

Ortiz writes his poems to be read aloud, and identifies more as a storyteller than a poet. He tries not to express his own interests in his work, but rather to write with the voice of the community. He has also tried to raise public awareness about Native American issues.

In 1993 the **Gift Festival of Native Writers** awarded Ortiz a Lifetime Achievement Award. He has published over twenty books of poetry and short fiction, and his work has influenced several other important writers, including **Joy Harjo** (see no. 96).

Academy Award–winning singer and song-writer **BUFFY SAINTE-MARIE** has spent much of her career celebrating the joys of Native American life and raising public awareness about the problems Native Americans face.

Sainte-Marie was born to **Cree** parents in Saskatchewan, Canada, and was adopted by a part-**Micmac** couple who raised her in Maine and Massachusetts. At the age of four, Sainte-Marie taught herself to play piano. As a child, she wrote songs easily, and as a teenager, she taught herself to play guitar.

After graduating from high school, she entered the University of Massachusetts. There, she played in coffeehouses and became known for love songs and songs about Native American life and social issues. In 1962 she completed her bachelor's degree; eventually she went on to earn a PhD as well.

Sainte-Marie moved to New York City and became part of the explosion of folk culture during the 1960s. She continued to sing in cafes and clubs, but she also released her first record in 1963, and the following year played her first **Carnegie Hall** concert. Critics noted her use of Native "vocables," meaningless syllables that are repeated in a tune, and her use of an ancient instrument, the mouthbow.

One critic praised her for her exceptional range, saying, "She can sing on, off, or around the pitch, as she chooses; her sense of phrasing is superb."

At about this time, Sainte-Marie became known as a Native American rights activist. Her song "Now That the Buffalo's Gone" is often called the first Native American protest song, and "Starwalker" has been called the theme song of the **American Indian Movement** (AIM). Sainte-Marie's song "Until It's Time" is one of the world's most recorded songs, with artists such as **Janis Joplin**, **Barbra Streisand**, and **Elvis Presley** among the hundreds who have recorded it.

During her career, Sainte Marie has traveled around the world and become internationally famous. In 1983 she received an Academy Award, a Golden Globe, and a Juno award for the song "Up Where We Belong." She has received a medal from Queen Elizabeth II, a Lifetime Achievement Award from the American Indian College Fund, and France's award for Best International Artist. Sainte-Marie is also an Officer of the Order of Canada, that nation's highest civilian honor.

In the late 1980s, Sainte-Marie pioneered a second career as a digital artist, creating paintings on a computer. She is an adjunct professor of fine arts at First Nations University of Canada. Her Cradleboard Teaching Project teaches Native American core curriculum online.

Sainte-Marie also continues to perform concerts and has released over fifteen albums.

FRANK DUKEPOO was the first **Hopi** to earn a PhD and at the time, became one of only a few Native Americans across the country to have a doctorate in the sciences.

Dukepoo grew up at First Mesa on the Mohave Reservation. He grew interested in genetics while listening to the advice of his father, a farmer, about where to plant seeds. In 1961 Dukepoo entered Arizona State University with several scholarships, but he lost them all when he let his grade point average fall below 1.2. Although racism was a problem on campus—Dukepoo remembered being called a "dirty, dumb, stupid, drunk Indian"—he said later that his biggest problem was that, like many college freshmen, "I had free time and money and didn't know what to do with it." However, one of his professors pushed him to pull his grades up, and he did—right up to 4.0. After earning his bachelor's degree, he continued his education and in 1973 graduated with a PhD in genetics.

Dukepoo held a variety of zoology and genetics-related jobs before joining the faculty of Northern Arizona University. In

addition to teaching biology, he directed a **National Science Foundation** program to encourage Native Americans at the university to stay in school. While he was the director, not a single student in the program dropped out.

Still, Dukepoo wanted to do more, and in 1982 he founded the **National Native American Honor Society**. To join, Native American students must have a 4.0 grade point average for at least one semester. By 1991 hundreds of students in the Southwest were members of NNAHS. Dukepoo also helped found two organizations devoted to encouraging minority students: the **Society for Advancement of Chicanos/Hispanics and Native Americans in Science** and the **American Indian Science and Engineering Society**.

At the same time, Dukepoo was conducting his own research. He researched birth defects among Southwestern Native Americans, and his study of albinism among the Hopi became a classic in the field. When the **Human Genome Project** began, Dukepoo was on the verge of mapping the gene for albinism among the Hopi.

However, he was concerned about what the Human Genome Project would mean to Native Americans, knowing that the scientific community historically has not always behaved ethically toward Native peoples. (For example, archaeologists have stolen bones from Native Americans, and doctors in the past have sterilized Native American women without their consent.)

So Dukepoo put his own research on hold. He began working with the Human Genome Project to make sure that indigenous peoples were treated ethically by researchers. But his work was cut short when he died suddenly of natural causes in 1999.

LEONARD PELTIER is one of the better-known federal prisoners in the United States. Since his controversial 1975 conviction for murdering two FBI agents, millions of people around the world have petitioned for his release.

Peltier, who is of **Ojibwa** and French descent, was born into a family of migrant workers. When he was four years old, his parents separated, and he went to live with his grandparents. With them, he moved back and forth between logging camps and copper mines.

When Peltier was about nine, a man drove up suddenly while he was outside playing. He recalls, "My grandmother started crying and told us this man was here to take us to Wahpeton Indian School." Peltier and his sister and cousin left for Wahpeton, where school officials cut their hair, stripped them, and poured powdered DDT on them. Peltier stayed at the boarding school until his mother could afford to care for him. Shortly afterward, he went to live with his father at the Turtle Mountain Reservation.

In 1959 Peltier moved to the Pacific Northwest. By the time he was twenty, he co-owned and operated an auto body shop in Seattle. He joined activists such as **Ramona Bennett** (see no. 85) to work on behalf of Northwest Native fishing rights. In the 1970s, he joined the **American Indian Movement** (AIM).

In 1972 Peltier got into an altercation with an off-duty policeman in Milwaukee and was charged with attempted murder. He jumped bail and went underground. Meanwhile, on South Dakota's **Pine Ridge Reservation,** some elders accused the tribal president, Dick Wilson, of corruption and of arming his own private police force. Violent incidents began to occur frequently, and the elders asked AIM for help. Peltier occupied the site of **Wounded Knee** on the reservation, along with **Dennis Banks** (see no. 82), **Clyde Bellecourt** (see no. 81), and other activists. Later, Peltier and others established a camp at the town of **Oglala** to protect people.

In 1975 two FBI agents drove toward the camp at Oglala, following Peltier and two other AIM activists, who were in a truck. There was a shoot-out, and someone shot both agents at close range, killing them. Peltier was tried and convicted of the murders and sentenced to two consecutive life terms in prison.

After the trial, there was an outpouring of support for Peltier. Dennis Banks, AIM, Amnesty International, and other groups have called for his release. Some of his supporters believe Peltier is innocent, and others believe he should be freed because there were irregularities in his trial. However, Peltier lost what may have been his best chance for freedom when outgoing President **Bill Clinton** refused to grant him a pardon in 2001. In 2017 President Barack Obama also refused to grant him clemency.

Despite his incarceration, Peltier published a book of essays in 1999 and even ran for president in 2004, representing the Peace and Freedom Party.

JOHN ECHOHAWK is a founder and executive director of the **Native American Rights Fund** (NARF), an organization that provides legal help to Native Americans and to Native American nations and organizations.

Echohawk was born in Albuquerque, New Mexico, to a distinguished **Pawnee** family. His grandfather was a scout for the U.S. Cavalry in the late 1800s; his uncle, painter and actor **Brummett Echohawk**, painted the famous picture *Trail of Tears*, which depicts the Cherokee as they were forced to relocate to Oklahoma during the 1830s.

John Echohawk grew up attending public school in New Mexico. He was one of six children, three of whom became lawyers. He came of age during the 1960s, and **Martin Luther King Jr.** became one of his heroes. After receiving a special scholarship to attend college from a new federal program for training Native lawyers, Echohawk became that program's first graduate. In law school, he cofounded the **American Indian Law Students Association**.

In 1970 Echohawk graduated from law school. That year, the Ford Foundation provided a grant to **California Indian Legal Services** (CILS) to establish a legal defense fund for Native Americans. CILS hired Echohawk to work on the project, and the Native American Rights Fund was born.

Echohawk transformed NARF into a powerful organization. As its executive director, he has supervised as many as fifty cases at a time, while also raising $7 million a year to pay for NARF's services. The organization has won hundreds of cases since its inception.

For example, in 1989 Echohawk won a case for the Catawba, enabling them to recover 144,000 acres of North Carolina land. In 1992 he won a federal district court case affirming the jurisdiction of tribal courts to hear civil matters on tribal lands in North Dakota. The same year, he forced Montana to recognize the Northern Cheyenne's right to ninety thousand acre-feet of water.

In 1996 NARF filed the largest class action suit ever against the federal government, demanding that the Bureau of Indian Affairs explain what happened to billions of dollars that it had held and managed for Native Americans during the last hundred years. The account is a trust fund comprising money paid by non-Natives to use Native land. According to the suit, the BIA did not know how much money had been collected and failed to "provide even a basic, regular statement to Indian account holders." Several years later, the case was still in the courts.

Echohawk has received many awards for his leadership in the field of law. The *National Law Journal* has named him one of the "100 Most Influential Lawyers in America," and the American Bar Association has given him its Spirit of Excellence Award.

WILMA MANKILLER was the first woman to be elected as principal chief of the **Cherokee** nation.

Mankiller was the sixth of eleven children in her family. The family lived on Cherokee land in Tahlequah, Oklahoma, in a four-room house that had no electricity and no running water. When she was ten years old, her family relocated to San Francisco. The experience was a tremendous culture shock for everyone.

In San Francisco, Mankiller graduated from high school, got married, and had two children. She also began working with Indian civil rights activists. Then in 1969, the American Indian Movement (AIM) and other activists occupied Alcatraz. Mankiller began to show her skill as an organizer, raising money and supplies for people participating in the occupation.

After the Alcatraz occupation ended, Mankiller threw herself into volunteer work with new energy. In 1974 she and her husband divorced, and she and her two daughters returned to Tahlequah. There, Mankiller began working for the Cherokee nation and attending college. In 1979 she was in a car accident that shattered her face, legs, and ribs. The driver of the other car, killed in the crash, was Mankiller's best friend.

After she recovered from the accident—and from a severe illness that required surgery and steroid therapy—Mankiller finally returned to her job with the Cherokee nation in 1980. One of her first projects was to organize volunteers and raise funds to build a water line for the town of Bell, which did not have running water and was one of the Cherokee's poorest communities.

In 1983 Cherokee chief **Ross Swimmer** asked Mankiller to run with him for reelection, as his deputy chief. Mankiller feared that people would think she was too liberal.

Instead, she received hate mail and death threats because of her gender. Mankiller later noted that the Cherokee had learned sexism from Europeans—traditionally, Cherokee women were always involved in government.

Swimmer and Mankiller won the election despite the controversy over her candidacy. In 1985 Swimmer resigned, and Mankiller became the first woman ever to be principal chief of the Cherokee nation. She narrowly won reelection in 1987 but got 82 percent of the vote in 1992.

As chief, Mankiller's job was to make sure that Cherokee laws were enforced, work with the tribal council to pass legislation, and supervise Cherokee-run programs. She spent much of her time writing grants for health and education programs, including the **Cherokee Home Health Agency** and **Head Start**.

Throughout her tenure as chief, Mankiller struggled with kidney disease. Then in 1995, Mankiller was diagnosed with lymphoma and did not run for reelection. In 1998 President Clinton awarded her the **Presidential Medal of Freedom**. She died of pancreatic cancer in 2010.

ROBERT EUGENE MEGGINSON, one of only a dozen Native Americans in the United States to have completed a doctoral degree in mathematics, has devoted much of his life to encouraging Native American students to study that subject.

Megginson grew up in a family that appreciated mathematics. His father, whose family was English, had a bachelor's degree in physics and math. His **Lakota** grandfather was very knowledgeable about mathematics and often gave him math problems to work out for fun.

At school, however, teachers and students sometimes were surprised if Megginson did not match their preconception of what a Native American should be like. Some teachers also lowered their expectations of Megginson because his family was not well off financially.

For example, though tests eventually showed that Megginson was about four grade levels ahead of his class, he was once placed in a remedial section of a class because the teacher assumed that a child with his background could not be a good student. Later, Megginson reflected that teachers all too often do lower their expectations in this way, sending a message—intentionally or not—that "because you are both American Indian and economically disadvantaged, you are doomed to do poorly in school." Fortunately, Megginson also encountered other teachers who recognized his abilities and encouraged him.

In college at the University of Illinois at Urbana-Champaign, Megginson did not immediately turn to mathematics. Initially, he completed a degree in physics and began working as a computer software specialist. However, in 1977 he decided to return to school, pursuing a master's degree in statistics and a PhD in mathematics. He became a teacher himself, first joining the faculty of Eastern Illinois University, and later that of the University of Michigan at Ann Arbor.

As a mathematician, Megginson has studied multidimensional spaces. In addition, he has worked to make it possible for other Native American students to follow in his footsteps. He is a member of several organizations that encourage minority participation in mathematics and often plans programs aimed at Native American students. In 1992 he developed a summer program for high school students at the Turtle Mountain Indian Reservation in North Dakota. The program stresses the connections between mathematics and traditional Ojibwa culture.

In 1997 Megginson received the **U.S. Presidential Award for Excellence in Science, Mathematics, and Engineering Mentoring.** In 1999 the American Indian Science and Engineering Society awarded him its Ely S. Parker Lifetime Achievement Award. He was named to the **Native American Science and Engineering Wall of Fame** in 2001. In 2012 he became a fellow of the American Mathematical Society.

LESLIE MARMON SILKO has been called "the most accomplished Indian writer of her generation," and is a major figure in the Native American renaissance that began in the 1960s.

Silko was born in Albuquerque, New Mexico, and raised on the **Old Laguna Pueblo Reservation**. She is of mixed ancestry, including Laguna Pueblo, Plains Pueblo, Mexican, and European heritage. Among the Laguna, women are important; Laguna women traditionally own property and Laguna gods are female. Not surprisingly, then, Silko was surrounded by strong female role models.

Her grandmother was a mechanic who fixed machines in her son's laundry even as an elderly woman. Her father encouraged Silko and her sisters to take part in traditionally male activities, such as hunting. Silko had her own horse by the time she was eight years old, and as a child helped round up the family's cattle.

Silko attended the local Bureau of Indian Affairs school as a child but commuted to a Catholic school in Albuquerque as a teenager. Then she attended the University of New Mexico. While there, she married and had a son. Busy as a parent, she decided to take a creative writing class she thought would give her an easy "A." It was the beginning of her career as a writer.

In 1971 Silko was awarded a grant from the **National Endowment for the Arts** based on a story she had originally written for class. By the time she received her NEA grant, she was in law school, but the grant convinced her to drop out and focus on her writing.

She began teaching at Navajo Community College in Tsaile, Arizona, and published a book of poems. Then she moved to Ketchikan, Alaska, where she wrote *Ceremony*, a book that is often compared to *House Made of Dawn*, **N. Scott Momaday's** Pulitzer Prize–winning novel. Both books concern a Native American veteran adjusting to life at home after World War II. *Ceremony* ends on a more optimistic note than does Momaday's novel, presenting Native traditions as a way to heal and regain one's sanity. In 1981 she released *Storyteller*, a collection of short stories and poems influenced by her experience with Laguna Pueblo storytelling, much like *Ceremony*.

After leaving Alaska, Silko returned to the Southwest, becoming a professor first at the University of New Mexico and then at the University of Arizona. During this time, she became friends with the poet **James Wright.** After Wright died of cancer, his widow published Silko's and Wright's letters to each other in *The Delicacy and Strength of Lace*, which won the prize for nonfiction from the *Boston Globe*.

In 1991 Silko was awarded a MacArthur Foundation fellowship, also known as a "genius grant." She used the money to support herself as she wrote her most controversial novel, *Almanac of the Dead*, which focuses on the history of genocide in the Americas. Since then, she has written several more books, including a novel, a collection of essays, and a memoir.

JOY HARJO is the first Native American to serve as **U.S. Poet Laureate** and is one of the foremost poets of the Native American literary renaissance. In addition to being a poet, she is a screenwriter, jazz musician, and teacher.

Harjo was born in Tulsa, Oklahoma, where her **Creek** ancestors had relocated when the federal government forced the Creek to give up their lands in Alabama and Georgia in the nineteenth century. An imaginative child, she pretended the oil wells in her neighborhood were monsters.

During her youth, Harjo hoped to become a missionary; she practiced preaching to the children of her neighborhood. However, she gave up her plans after she watched her local minister ask two Mexican girls to leave church because they were too noisy. She left with them and didn't go back.

When she was sixteen, Harjo began attending a boarding school, the **Institute of American Indian Arts** (IAIA), in Santa Fe, New Mexico. There, she took up painting, and after hearing readings by **Leslie Marmon Silko** (see no. 95) and **Simon J. Ortiz** (see no. 88), she was also inspired to begin writing poetry. Then she went on to college—at the University of New Mexico at Albuquerque, where she studied painting and creative writing.

Harjo also had her two children while studying there, in 1968 and 1973. To support

herself and them, she worked as a waitress, gas-station attendant, and nurse's assistant. After graduating, Harjo earned her master's in fine arts from the University of Iowa and began teaching at universities, including the University of Arizona and the University of New Mexico.

During her years of teaching, Harjo was also writing poetry. She published several books of poetry, and her 1983 volume, *She Had Some Horses,* remained in print for more than a decade and is often used in college literature courses. She has often written about the history of exploitation and oppression in the Americas, including both the Native American genocide and the Reconstruction-era lynching of African Americans.

When she was in her thirties, Harjo began teaching herself to play the saxophone with the help of **Jim Pepper**, a Creek/Kaw jazz saxophonist. She began playing soprano and alto saxophone with an all–Native American band called **Poetic Justice**. The band's music accompanied Harjo's readings of her poetry on a CD that accompanied the 1994 edition of her book *The Woman Who Fell from the Sky*. She has recorded many other solo albums.

Harjo continued writing and publishing her poetry to great acclaim, including her collections *How We Became Human* in 2004, *Conflict Resolution for Holy Beings* in 2015, and *An American Sunrise* in 2019. Her poetry often reflects on colonialism and imperialism and their effect on women. She has received many awards for her poetry, including the William Carlos Williams Award of the **Poetry Society of America**, and the Lifetime Achievement Award from the **Native Writers Circle of the Americas**. In 2019 she became the first Native American to be named U.S. Poet Laureate and became only the second person ever to serve at least three terms in the role.

LOUISE ERDRICH is an award-winning writer, poet, and author of over thirty books and is considered one of the most widely acclaimed Native American writers of her time. Part-**Ojibwa**, she is best known for the books she has written portraying life among the Ojibwa, including *Love Medicine*, *The Beet Queen, The Round House*, *The Bingo Palace,* and *LaRose*.

Erdrich grew up in Wahpeton, a town near the North Dakota and Minnesota border. Her parents taught in Bureau of Indian Affairs schools, and they encouraged Erdrich to write. Her father paid her a nickel for each story she finished, and her mother bound the stories into little books with construction paper covers.

Erdrich was raised Catholic and attended Catholic public schools, but she learned about Ojibwa traditions from her grandfather. Although he was also Catholic, Erdrich has said that he went into the woods, not church, to pray and that he prayed in Ojibwa. Once, she said, her grandfather told her that he was praying for a safe landing on the moon. She admired his ability to combine traditional practices with modern life.

Erdrich entered Dartmouth College in 1972, part of the first class of women admitted to the school. After completing her degree in English, she took any job she could find that would allow her time to write—selling popcorn at movie theaters, working as a lifeguard, or waitressing.

In 1979 she completed a master's degree in fine arts at Johns Hopkins University and began writing fiction and editing the newspaper of the **Boston Indian Council**. In 1981 she married Michael Dorris, a writer and scholar she had met while he was teaching at Dartmouth.

Erdrich's relationship with Dorris helped both of them become more productive in

their literary careers. They collaborated on most of their works, with one writing a first draft of a piece and the other reading it over and commenting on it. Dorris also acted as an agent for Erdrich's first book, *Love Medicine*, which won the **National Book Critics Circle Award** in 1984. The couple separated in 1995, and in 1997 Dorris died by suicide, after two of their children accused him of abuse.

Erdrich continued writing prolifically after Dorris's death, winning prestigious awards and wide recognition. Her children's book *The Birchbark House* (1999) and her novel *The Last Report on the Miracles at Little No Horse* (2001) were both National Book Award finalists. In 2009 she was a Pulitzer Prize finalist for her book *The Plague of Doves,* and *The Round House* won the National Book Award for fiction in 2012. Erdrich also owns and operates Birchbark Books, a small independent bookstore in Minneapolis that specializes in Native literature, art, and gifts.

U.S. Naval aviator and engineer **JOHN BENNETT HERRINGTON** became the first enrolled member of a Native American tribe to fly in space.

Herrington was born into the **Chickasaw Nation** in Wetumka, Oklahoma. During his childhood, his family moved often, living in Colorado, Wyoming, and Texas, where Herrington graduated from high school. He dreamed of becoming an astronaut and entered college but was suspended after an unsuccessful first year, preferring rock climbing to academic responsibilities. He soon found work utilizing his rock-climbing skills on a survey crew in the Colorado mountains. In this work, he discovered a passion for real-world applications of math, which inspired him to return to college. He graduated from the University of Colorado at Colorado Springs in 1983 with a degree in applied mathematics.

After graduation, Herrington joined the navy and in 1984 received his commission from Aviation Officer Candidate School and became a naval aviator in 1985. He attended Naval Test Pilot School, graduating in 1990, and completed a master of science degree in aeronautical engineering in 1995.

In 1996 Herrington was selected by **NASA**. He qualified as a mission specialist for flight assignment after two years of training and served as a member of the team responsible for shuttle launch and post-landing operations. In 2002 he traveled to the International Space Station in the space shuttle STS-113 *Endeavor*, becoming the first Native American to accomplish space flight and a space walk. In honor of his heritage, Herrington brought the flag of the Chickasaw Nation, eagle feathers, wooden flutes, and other meaningful items with him on the thirteen-day mission.

Herrington retired from the navy and NASA in 2005, and in 2008 he completed a three-month, 4,300-mile cross-country bike ride, starting in Cape Flattery, Washington, and ending in Cape Canaveral, Florida. Later, he completed a PhD in education at the University of Idaho and even published a children's book about astronaut training called *Mission to Space*, which includes an English-to-Chickasaw list of space terms. He was one of the first inductees into the National Native American Hall of Fame in 2018.

Activist and writer **WINONA LADUKE** has twice run as the **Green Party** candidate for the office of vice president of the United States.

LaDuke grew up on the West Coast. Her mother, a Jewish art professor, and her father, an **Ojibwa** actor, were both antiwar activists during the Vietnam War, leading LaDuke to become interested in politics at an early age.

As a teenager, LaDuke began studying the impact of mining and multinational corporations on reservations. When she was eighteen, she presented her research before the United Nations. Afterward, she alternated between her studies at Harvard University and work on reservations. Eventually LaDuke graduated from Harvard with degrees in Native economic development and rural development.

After graduating, she moved to the area her family came from—the White Earth Reservation in northern Minnesota. She became the principal for the **Circle of Life** School on the reservation and began working on a lawsuit to recover Ojibwa lands from the logging industry and the federal government. When the lawsuit failed, LaDuke founded the **White Earth Land Recovery Project**, an organization that buys back Ojibwa lands an acre at a time. To begin the project, she used the money from the **Reebok Human Rights Award**, which she won in 1989.

In 1994 *Time* magazine named LaDuke one of America's fifty most promising leaders under the age of forty. In 1996 the Green Party asked her to run for president of the United States. She refused but did agree to run for vice president as consumer advocate **Ralph Nader's** running mate. The two headed the Green Party ticket once again in the 2000 election.

In 2000 she campaigned while nursing a baby, her third child. Although Nader and LaDuke won only one percent of the vote in 1996, they may have changed the outcome of the 2000 election when they drew almost three percent of the national vote, and in some states, such as Oregon and California, even higher totals.

Many analysts believe that Nader and LaDuke attracted many left-leaning voters who would otherwise have voted for Democrat Al Gore, and that resulted in Republican George W. Bush winning the election. More importantly for their supporters, Nader and LaDuke catapulted the Green Party into national prominence, making it a viable third-party option in many states. In the 2016 presidential election, though she wasn't running, LaDuke received one electoral college vote from a Washington State elector.

Outside of elections, LaDuke has devoted much of her time to research, writing, and activism, including participating in the protests against the Dakota Access Pipeline in 2016, which were heavily covered by national media at the time. She has written countless articles on Native American issues and the environment; a novel, *Last Standing Woman* (1997); and multiple nonfiction books, including *All Our Relations* (1999, updated 2016), *Reclaiming the Sacred* (2005), and *The Militarization of Indian Country* (2013). She has also coauthored more than ten other nonfiction books. In 1998 *Ms.* magazine named her "Woman of the Year." In 2007 she was inducted into the National Women's Hall of Fame.

DEB HAALAND, an enrolled member of the **Laguna Pueblo**, was one of the first Native American women elected to the U.S. Congress and became the first Native American to serve as a cabinet secretary.

Born in 1960, Haaland grew up in a military family, moving frequently—her Native American mother served in the navy, and her Norwegian Minnesotan father was an officer in the marine corps. She attended thirteen public schools across the country before her family settled down in New Mexico close to her Laguna Pueblo family. After graduating from high school and working for several years, Haaland attended the University of New Mexico, giving birth to her daughter just four days after graduating with her bachelor's degree in 1994. She was a single mother and struggled to afford housing for herself and her daughter, and started a small business, producing and canning salsa in an effort to support herself. She also volunteered at her daughter's preschool to make it more affordable.

She attended law school at the University of New Mexico and earned her JD in 2006. She served as the Tribal Administrator for the San Felipe Pueblo from 2013 to 2015 and was the first chairwoman elected to the Laguna Development Corporation Board of Directors. In her role as chairwoman, she successfully argued for environmentally friendly business practices by the company, which was the second largest tribal gaming enterprise in New Mexico.

Haaland ran for New Mexico lieutenant governor in 2014. Though she lost, she was elected as the chair of the **Democratic Party of New Mexico** in 2015, making her the first Native American woman to lead a state party. During her two-year term as chair, she raised enough money to pay off the debt that had accumulated during the prior seven years.

In 2018 Haaland was elected to the U.S. House of Representatives, becoming one of the first two Native American women, (the other being Sharice Davids) to win seats in Congress. Haaland wore moccasins and traditional pueblo dress to her 2019 swearing-in ceremony. She won her reelection in 2020 but was shortly thereafter nominated by President Joe Biden to serve as **secretary of the interior**. She was confirmed by the Senate in March 2021, becoming the first Native American cabinet secretary in U.S. history. Her appointment to the Department of the Interior was also especially significant because it marked the first time in history that a Native American led the department that oversees the **Bureau of Indian Affairs**, the federal agency that implements laws related to American Indians and provides services to the two million Native Americans in the United States.

TRIVIA QUESTIONS

Test your knowledge and challenge your friends. The answers are contained in the biographies noted.

1. Which early seventeenth-century Native American helped bring peace between her people and the first English settlers in America? (See no. 4)

2. Which eighteenth-century Iroquois founded a new religion that is still practiced by many of his people today? (See no. 9)

3. How did a Native American create a system of writing for the Cherokee language that became universally adopted by the entire Cherokee nation? (See no. 15)

4. Who was the Native American woman who served as a guide to the explorers Lewis and Clark on their journey to explore the Louisiana Purchase? (See no. 17)

5. Where did the famous Seminole leader Osceola lead his people's resistance against the U.S. government's efforts to relocate them? (See no. 21)

6. Who was the first—and last—Native American leader in the West to win a war against the U.S. government? (See no. 29)

7. When did the most famous battle in history between Native Americans and the U.S. military take place? (See no. 35)

8. How did a famous Nez Percé chief lead his people on the most brilliant retreat in the history of Native American and U.S. military warfare? (See no. 40)

9. When was the first Native American elected to the U.S. Senate? (See no. 50)

10. Which Native American pitcher is a member of the Baseball Hall of Fame? (See no. 56)

11. Who was the first Native American to receive the Presidential Medal of Freedom? (See no. 63)

12. Why did a World War II hero's act of bravery ultimately cause him to be remembered as "a hero to everyone but himself?" (See no. 69)

13. Which Native American was the first U.S. ballerina to become internationally famous? (See no. 72)

14. Which writer became the first Native American to win the Pulitzer Prize for fiction? (See no. 79)

15. Who became the first American athlete to win a long distance track event at the Olympic Games? (See no. 84)

16. Why did activists of the American Indian Movement occupy the site of Wounded Knee on the Pine Ridge Reservation in 1972? (See no. 91)

PROJECT SUGGESTIONS

1. Choose one Native American tribe described in several of the biographies. Read as many entries as necessary in order to write a two- or three-paragraph essay about the tribe. Describe where the tribe made its home and who its most famous leaders were. Provide details about the relations the tribe had with the U.S. government over a prolonged period of time. Were there many conflicts or wars? How were they resolved? Were relations peaceful? Was the tribe eventually relocated, and did they accept relocation peacefully or engage in a fight against it? In your essay, also describe what happened to one or two of the tribe's most notable leaders.

2. Choose one of the people from this book and write a one-page fictional diary entry for one day in that person's life. Pick a day that had some significance for the individual; for example, the day he or she received a significant award or achieved some other noteworthy success. Or choose a day on which the person met with a personal setback or was frustrated in some way by a lack of success. Describe the person's thoughts and feelings with as much detail as you can.

3. Many lands were home to native and indigenous peoples long before they were colonized by newcomers from other countries. Ask an adult to help you look up your current location on native-land.ca. Research the tribe or peoples who originally owned the land, and write one page about them. What are some important events in their history? Who are their most notable individuals?

INDEX

OUT NOW: